Practising
Yoga

AND SPIRIT

Practising Yoga

MIND · BODY AND SPIRIT ·

GEDDES & GROSSET

Published by Geddes & Grosset,
David Dale House, New Lanark ML11 9DJ, Scotland

© 1999 Geddes & Grosset

Published 1999, reprinted 1999, 2001

Cover image courtesy of the Telegraph Colour Library

ISBN 1 85534 377 0

Printed and bound in the UK

Contents

Chapter One

What is Yoga?

Stop what you are doing. Stand up, take a deep breath and have a really good stretch. Standing on tiptoes, make yourself as tall as possible with your hands reaching up to the sky and your fingers splayed. Breathe out slowly, and slowly resume your normal standing posture. Now doesn't that feel good? Can you feel the blood tingling in your hands and feet? Do the muscles in your arms and legs feel relaxed and yet energised? Does your mind, be it only for a fleeting moment, seem to have taken a breather from its daily round of thoughts and worries? If your answer is yes, then you are feeling the benefits of yoga already.

Yoga is a system of physical and mental exercises designed to instill a sense of tranquillity and wellbeing in the practitioner. Its origins are lost in the mists of time, though estimates suggest that it has been practised in India for over five thousand years, and is believed to have been inspired by the contemplation of animals, particularly cats, as they stretched. Observers noted that, after a good stretch and arch, the animal's energy and alertness was increased, and so they sought to utilize this knowledge for human benefit. To this day, many yoga positions are named after the creatures they were adapted from: the tortoise, the cobra, the butterfly.

Yoga, a Sanskrit word, means to 'yoke or harness', and is the root of the English verb 'to yoke'. Yoga seeks to harness the energy of the body and mind and use it more beneficially. Think for a moment of the amount of time we waste energy, in worry and anger, in sleeplessness and fidgeting, and how wonderful it would be to channel that energy into something more useful. Think of the novels, the theses, the exercise regimes, the plans and initiatives, that are abandoned by people who find their energies dissipated by countless other, often very minor, concerns. How wonderful it would be to rein in all that energy and focus it on the task in hand!

Yoga also means 'union', referring to the union of body and mind that practise seeks to achieve. By uniting the two, yoga helps to control negative and destructive thought patterns and assist the mind to work with, rather than against, the body. Increasingly we are learning the importance of the mind in matters of the body. Research is revealing that ailments as various as obesity and cancer have links to the mindstate of the patient, and that the orthodox medical system of curing the body alone, without taking into consideration mental and emotional factors, is flawed. The old maxim that 'A healthy body is a healthy mind' has never seemed so true. In short, feeling good makes us well.

The first text

The first written yoga system is the *Yoga Sutras* of Pantajali, dating from around 200 to 400 BC. Written in the ancient language of Sanskrit, Pantajali's text is the earliest collation and systematisation of an ancient knowledge that was previously handed down in the oral tradition. The *Yoga Sutras* are not advised as a teach yourself companion, as they are extremely complex, but rather as a guide for teachers to adapt.

According to Pantajali, yoga brings about the suspension of the mind's waves (*vrittis*), resulting in mindfulness, which means the ability to pay attention to your life. To put it in modern terminology, to 'wake up and smell the coffee' or 'get real'. This means experiencing what is happening around and within you, rather than being consumed by internal mental convolutions while life passes you by. To avoid the situation as described by W.H. Auden: '*In headaches and in worry/Vaguely life leaks away.*'

To achieve these, Pantajali advocates practice (*abhaysa*) and non-attachment (*vairagya*). The latter does not necessitate the abandonment of all worldly goods, but a relinquishment of assumptions about yourself and the world. Consider how many times you duck opportunities because you are 'not right for it', either because you feel you are not capable of it, or because it is not suited to you. Many modern psychologists would tell us, in no uncertain terms, that we are wrong in these self-judgements, and that in fact we do not really know ourselves at all. Our beliefs are often based upon a hotchpotch of experience (often misleading), upon other people's opinions, and our fears and prejudices. If this seems absurd, consider the re-action of children to new experiences: curious, eager and positive, they embrace the unknown, unhindered by accumulated memories and assumptions. Experience, in a sense, actually blinkers us to the world, and hobbles our development.

Yoga and religion

The *Upanishads*, the ancient sacred books outlining the mystical and esoteric doctrines of Hindu philosophy, and dating from around 500 BC, make much reference to yoga. The initial effects of practice are described as a feeling of 'lightness' and a clearer complexion – two greatly desired states in the modern world. However, the ultimate goal is to achieve *samadhi*, a higher consciousness that is characterised by a feeling of oneness with the universe. Ego is transcended and the individual self (*atman*) becomes one with the universal self (*brahman*).

The *Bhagavad Gita*, perhaps the most famous text, dating from 300 to 400 BC, describes yoga as the means to achieving enlightenment, in the context of the Hindu tradition of spiritual discipline. However, Hinduism is by no means intrinsic to yoga. All world religions seek to reintegrate the worshipper with the supreme being, and yoga practitioners of all denominations report an increased sense of their own spirituality thanks to the disciplines of yoga. It is all too easy to worship by rote, saying the prayers, reading the texts, observing the duties, without experiencing the joy of faith and a feeling of union with the creator. Yoga enables many to do this.

Of course, yoga does not require religious belief at all, which is one of the reasons why it will be around for a long, long time to come. More and more people are turning away from orthodox religion, and instead are seeking to discover a personal sense of spirituality – their own bespoke religion, if you like, based on personally felt tenets of belief. Yoga is an excellent means of tapping into this.

Even if spirituality is not something that interests you, yoga is also beneficial in enhancing your enjoyment of the present. To be absorbed in an activity, like a child becomes when playing a game or drawing, is to experience it fully, and thus to wring every last drop of enjoyment from it. Who ever thoroughly felt the exhilaration of a cross-country canter, or the melancholy beauty of a sunset, while their mind was worrying over an overdraft or an future job interview? Yoga teaches you to 'let go', to filter out distractions and just be.

Chapter Two

The Six Paths
and the Eight Limbs

The six paths of yoga
Samadhi, or self-realisation, can be reached by six different strands of yoga, though some are less open to secular interpretation than others. There is, however, no requirement to subscribe to all six paths.

Bhakti yoga
Bhakti yoga is characterised by devotion. To achieve the ultimate goal, the Bhakti practitioner must meditate upon the supreme being, and behave unselfishly towards his or her fellow man. As in countless religions, yoga advocates that you love your neighbour; a universal message for promoting harmony. Most of us are already aware of the inner sense of joy engendered by doing completely unselfish acts.

Gyana yoga
Gyana (or jnana) yoga is concerned with wisdom, and

urges the study of texts as well as a deep consideration of the questions of life, such as who we are and why we are here. Followers are pointed towards the *Bhagavad Gita* and other sacred texts, to search for meaning therein, just as medieval monks poured over the gospels, seeking new insights.

Karma yoga

Karma yoga is the yoga of actions. Just as Giotto held that his frescoes were, in themselves, an act of worship, so the Karma subscriber seeks to praise his creator through thought and deed, and to regard his or her work as an act of worship.

Mantra yoga

Mantra yoga utilizes sound. The mantra yogi concentrates his mind on the divine by constantly repeating a sound or mantra. This sound need not be uttered allowed; internal mantras are just as effective. The best known mantra is Om, the sacred Sanskrit syllable used by many Hindus in their meditations. The practice of using sound to focus the mind is used in many religions, including Hare Krishna, where the repetition of the words Hare and Krishna are used to induce a trancelike meditative state in which the oneness of creation is felt. In a secular context, Mahareshi Mahesh's Transcendental Meditation (TM) also uses a mantra, given to a TM student by his/her teacher.

Hatha yoga

Hatha yoga is the only physical yoga and the one that this book mostly concentrates upon. It is the strand that most people take up first, or indeed, exclusively. Hatha yoga seeks to strengthen the inner as well as outer body, that is, the internal organs as well as the external muscles, and to focus the mind through physical activity.

Hatha yoga is considered by some as merely the necessary preliminary to raja yoga. The idea is that the body must be at its healthiest and strongest if you are to achieve transcendence. This does not, however, mean that your body must conform to an ideal of physical beauty, but that it should be as good as it can be. Thus disability or age need not be a hindrance.

Raja yoga

The word 'raja' means king, so raja yoga is the king, or ultimate, of yogas. This kind of yoga cleanses and strengthens the mind that has already been focused through Hatha practice. When the mind is at its most pure, all distractions banished, inspirations come and problems that once seemed insurmountable, are solved. The deeply relaxed state induced by Raja is sometimes referred to as the Alpha state, a level of consciousness somewhere between waking and sleep, when the mind is free and at its peak of creativity.

Practising Yoga

All six yogas seek to unite the self and the universe. Though they may look solitary, the text studying, the silent repetition of mantras, they produce a sense of belonging that is the very antithesis of solitude.

The eight limbs

Most people who take up yoga find that, after a while, it begins to have an effect upon their lifestyle and codes of behaviour, as they begin to take more and more control of their destinies. The eight limbs of yoga, first spelled out in Pantajali's *Yoga Sutras*, provide guidelines for yoga lifestyle as well as practice.

The limbs are abstinences (*yamas*), observances (*niyamas*), postures (*asanas*), breath control (*pranayama*), withdrawal of senses (*pratyahara*), concentration (*dharana*), meditation (*dhyana*) and self-realisation (*samadhi*).

It is important to be aware that yoga is not a system cast in stone. Adapt its ideas to suit your own, just as you will learn to adapt the postures of hatha yoga to suit your levels of strength and suppleness.

The abstinences (*yamas*)
Nonviolence (*ahisma*)

The first of these is the principle of nonviolence (*ahisma*), which is not merely a directive to not administer bodily pain. You may be someone who has never raised their hand to anyone, but be violent with words, wreaking emotional rather than physical havoc. You may be violent towards the environment, doing your bit to spread pollution, or violent towards yourself, either in extreme forms, such as self-mutilation, or in self-destructive habits, such as bulimia nervosa, or alcoholism.

Ahisma is not a passive principle; indeed, it can require enormous creativity and energy finding nonviolent ways to achieve ends that may previously have been reached with violence, or the threat of it.

Truthfulness (satya)

The second yama is that of truthfulness (*satya*). This is not just about not telling lies, but about living with integrity. This can mean not talking about someone behind their back and being honest about personally held convictions. It does not mean speaking your mind, however cruelly, in the manner of the Jim Carrey character in the film *Liar, Liar* (which tells the story of a lawyer who suddenly loses his ability to deal in half-truths and cannot stop himself from blurting out exactly what he thinks, no matter what the situation). There are times when a white lie is actually more honourable than a truth.

Non-stealing (asteya)

Next is non-stealing (*asteya*), which is against taking anything that is not rightfully yours, including the credit for something you do not deserve, or stealing someone's time, by demanding their attention and support to an unfair degree. Only you can judge when the line has been crossed. All yoga principles leave the responsibility firmly up to the individual, which may at first seem like a burden, but is, in fact, incredibly liberating.

Continence (bramachanya)

The fourth yama is that of continence (*bramachanya*). This is often interpreted as meaning celibacy, which it does not; rather it is a principle of moderation in all things. Avoid being the slave of your desires. The 1990s have seen the concept of addiction as a disease hit the headlines. Unfortunately, the underlying message in these media stories is that addicts cannot control themselves, whether their addiction be to Class A drugs or having sex with strangers. Yoga does not accept this; you are in charge of your appetites and it is your job to keep a rein on them. It goes without saying that you should avoid tempting others to overindulge themselves either.

Non-possessiveness (aparigrapha)

Non-possessiveness (*aparigrapha*) is the final yama, and requires you to free yourself from materialism. In the 1980s, many people discovered that materialism did not make them happy. Indeed, many found the opposite to be the case, as they substituted the pursuit of wealth for other values, leaving them with a feeling of emptiness despite their materialistic ambitions being realised. Aparigrapha does not require the relinquishing of comfort and wealth, simply that you begin to value it less highly and turn your attention to less worldly matters.

The principle also requires living without envying what others have, whether it be acres of land or a perfect hour-glass figure.

The observances (*niyamas*)
Purity (*saucha*)

Purity (*saucha*) requires the cleanliness of the internal and external body, as well as of the mind. Before practising yoga postures, you are advised to shower and wear clean clothes. To cleanse the inner body, yogics advised a pure (*sattvic*) diet and *pranayama*, a system of breathing that helps to clean out the system.

Purifying the mind is an altogether more difficult matter, as it involves the clearing out of old resentments and prejudices, just as you would clear out an old cupboard. However, like the cupboard, a cleared-out mind has acres of room for new ideas and progress. Modern therapy practices agree with the idea that mental detritus hinders clear thought and can stop you from moving forward in life, and that unresolved emotions can fester and become deeply negative. For instance, unresolved anger can turn into bitterness, isolation to insecurity.

In future, resolve to deal with emotional situations as they arise, and avoid repeating behavioural patterns that result in negative feelings. This does not mean flying off the handle, but recognising strong emotions such as anger, and choosing how to respond. Nor does it mean cowering away from life, but simply recognising and avoiding destructive situations.

Contentment (santosha)

Contentment (*santosha*) urges you to be happy with your lot, to rid yourself of desires and accept the hand that fate has dealt you. If this sounds like an invitation to abdicate responsibility for the direction your life will take, consider it another way. The ancients were well aware that bad days came as often as good ones, that no-one who ever lived avoided at least some tragedy and unhappiness. Santosha would be better seen as an acknowledgement of each moment that makes up your life. After all, not one of them will come again, and even bad times are unique. Also, there is no peace to be found in denying or resisting pain. Consider the story of Jean-Dominique Bauby, one-time editor of French *Elle*, who, following a stroke, became a victim of 'locked-in' syndrome, a debility which robbed him of all faculties of movement and speech. He wrote an account of his illness, and his coming to terms with it, called *The Diving Bell and The Butterfly*, by dictating it letter for letter using his the movement of his eyelashes by way of communication. By accepting his new state, living with it rather than railing mentally against it, Bauby came to find a sense of profound peace. Had he instead continued to compare his present to his past, he would have experienced the remainder of his life as a period of unmitigated torment.

Santosha also advises against denying your present through daydreaming and fantasy; 'wishing your life away', in other words. Far better to be fully alive to your life as it happens.

Austerity (tapas)

Austerity (*tapas*) has nothing to do with horsehair shirts or kneeling on cold stone floors, but is merely the observance of discipline and simplicity. Such a lifestyle will assist you in sticking to your purpose, rather than being snared by the distractions of a complicated existence. The novelist Anne Fine, author of *Mrs Doubtfire,* described, in an interview in *The Guardian,* the moment she realised how to achieve success as a writer. She was changing the bedsheets one day, and happened to be listening to a play on the radio. One of the actors said the words 'Simplify, simplify', and she realised that this was what she needed to do with her life. From that day forth, she filtered out all the unnecessary little tasks that used up her energy and thoughts and devoted herself to what she truly burned to do.

The word 'tapas' comes from 'tap', meaning to burn or blaze. Observance of tapas will allow your inner light to burn all the more brightly.

Study (svadhyaya)
Study (*svadhyaya*) requires the study of life and its meaning, and any study or activity that increases knowledge of the self. This latter could include voluntary work or spending time with the elderly or children, interacting with the world in such a way that untried, even unsuspected, aspects of the self are brought out. It also requires a certain degree of solitariness and thoughtfulness, giving you time to listen to how your own mind ticks, as well as to contemplate the workings of the world around you.

Attentiveness to the divine (ishvara pranidhana)
Attentiveness to the divine (*ishvara pranidhana*) is the transcending of the ego, as you seek to become one with the supreme being. To achieve this, short-termism must be abandoned in favour of the long-term, your energies and thoughts devoted to the pursuit of love, progress and creation, Ishvara, not dissipated by day-to-day issues and wants.

The *asanas* will be detailed in Chapter Four, and *pranayama* and the final four limbs of yoga explained in Chapter Eight, which looks at meditation.

Chapter Three

Yoga and Healing

Over two millennia ago the Bhudda said, 'You are what you think.' Today, as we become less and less enchanted with the side-effects of modern medicine, we are taking on board this ancient wisdom. Homeopathy is rising in popularity as it is based on the principle of invoking the body's natural healing properties rather than overriding them to quell symptoms.

This propensity of the body's to heal and strengthen itself is sometimes called the 'life force'. The force of this flow can be stemmed by a failure to respond to our body's needs, in diet, exercise, mental stability. However, it is a powerful force and remains undaunted even after years of abuse. If it wasn't so strong, then those who neglect their diet and prefer alcohol to green tea would not stand a chance in the face of serious infection.

Yoga not only tones and strengthens muscles, it also tones and strengthens the mind, making you feel that you are more in control of your life, which is often half the battle when it comes to staving off, and fighting, infection.

Practising Yoga

We all know that placebos can sometimes effectively 'cure' a complaint, simply by the power of suggestion. The mysterious cures that occur at shrines such as Lourdes and Assisi, have also been attributed, by some doctors and psychologists, to the power of the pilgrim's mind rather than the workings of the divine. Meanwhile newspapers and magazines report scores of incredible reversals in seemingly terminal cases, each and every one caused by the sufferer's determination to be well. They may say it was because they could not abandon their children, or were too young to die. But what they had done was take control of their illness and thereby control of their life, directing them where they wanted to go. Similarly, it is very difficult to cure someone who has 'lost the will to live.' When we someone is 'fighting for their life' we are not referring to a physical battle, but to a struggle of the mind to overcome matter.

Yoga and stress

The latter half of the 20th century is a time of vastly accelerated culture. We see more changes in a decade than our nineteenth-century ancestors witnessed in a lifetime. We crave faster and faster transport and communications, are urged to meet tighter and tighter deadlines, and attempt to relax at an equally breakneck pace, with high-impact aerobics, or thrill-seeking sports. Even our children are fast-tracked, spurred on to display academic abilities at increasingly younger ages, and to plan their careers and future lifestyles when they are barely in their teens. No wonder we all feel as if there is no time to lose, despite the fact that we can now expect to live longer than ever before.

A little bit of stress is essential. Without it we simply wouldn't make deadlines and nothing would prompt us into action. An athlete could never win a race if he did not experience a sufficient degree of stress to make him push himself to the limit.

Too much unrelieved pressure, however, can destroy our mental and physical health. It can lead to heart disease, ulcers and hypertension, as well as depression and even suicide. Of course too little to do creates a different kind of pressure and can be damaging too, as unemployed and retired people discover when they suddenly find themselves without purpose and oceans of time on their hands. Many people who have 'lived' for their work, such as self-employed businessmen, die quite shortly after retiring as they have no facility for coping with idleness and become terribly stressed.

If we take on too much work, or even overcommit ourselves socially so that we are running from pillar to post trying to fulfil all our promises, we become stressed as we struggle to meet unrealistic deadlines. Alternatively, if we feel that life is passing us by, and that we have nothing to contribute, we also become stressed. Our hearts race, we become 'locked' into anxiety, and find it impossible to relax.

This heart racing is caused by our adrenaline kicking in. In response to danger, our bodies operate a 'fight or flight' response, pumping adrenaline through the nervous system which stimulates the muscles into action whilst temporarily shutting down secondary processes such as digestion. This 'fight or flight' response dates from the time when we carried spears and ran away from sabre tooth tigers. The adrenaline would naturally disperse as we hared off over the hills, and our digestion and heart rate would return to normal.

Unfortunately, if all this is happening while we are trapped behind a computer, with no hope of heading for the hills till at least the small hours of the morning, the adrenaline remains where it is, unused, which can be very harmful. All that blood sugar, coursing through the veins to pump the muscles full of energy, has nowhere to go. The result can be congested arteries, which effectively narrows them, forcing the heart to work harder at pumping blood through the body. Too much of this, and the final result can be admittance to the cardiac ward.

Combating the problem of stress is turning into a multi-million-dollar industry. Large corporations are drafting in aromatherapists, hypnotists and stress gurus to calm down their staff and keep them in work. Companies annually report one of their biggest losses as being due to staff absence, which is increasing, and increasingly caused by stress-related illness. Shops are overflowing with cassettes of waves and whales, scented candles and crystals, books and charts and pamphlets, all designed to help you unwind. Many of these work of course, but the method that comes with a stamp of approval from many doctors, who suggest it to heart disease and hypertension patients, is yoga.

The reason yoga works so effectively in the war to reduce stress is that, because it requires absorption, the mind is diverted from sources of anxiety. With regular practice you will begin to know your true self – not the one who attends meetings or has clocked up 10,000 air miles, but the essence of your being. This self-knowledge will lend you a deep-rooted confidence that will enable you to reorder your priorities in such a way that you are not permanently exhausted or missing out in the good things in life. It will help you to be assertive, but not aggressive, generous but not a doormat, and content without being complacent.

It can also bring about increased communion with, and respect for, your body, the desire for artificial stimulants lessens (after a few months of yoga, many smokers quit with relative ease), as does the tendency to eat whatever is convenient and skip exercise because you are too tired. Yoga will help you to be less tired as its ability to reduce anxiety will result in more restful sleep.

This new wellbeing is lasting, and can help to reverse the effects of even serious complaints, like heart disease, and can reduce the signs of aging. As one centenarian responded when asked the secret of long life: 'It's simple. Good food and no worries.'

Breaking addictions

Few of us reach adulthood without being addicted to something, whether it be high tar cigarettes, intense physical exercise (or rather, the hormones released into the brain by bouts of physical exercise, causing a sensation of being 'high'), chocolate biscuits or constant cups of coffee. What all addictions have in common is that we feel we need them in order to maintain our equilibrium. Smokers find that they feel afraid at the idea of running out of cigarettes, while jogging addicts panic if they cannot go out for a run. The fact is, of course, that they do not need these things at all, and that the continued addiction is actually doing their body harm in the long term.

They know that, after the initial withdrawal symptoms, the body will feel fine, if not markedly better than before. However, it is not the physical side of the addiction that is so insidious; it is the psychological side. Nine times out of ten, when a smoker announces that they are 'dying for a smoke', they are not responding to a physical symptom, but a psychological one. They regard the cigarette as an emotional prop, something that will make them feel more relaxed perhaps, or more confident, and the belief that it will do so continues no matter how many times it fails to live up to its promise.

Beating addiction, once and for all, is a huge step and requires enormous effort. Yoga has helped many people to break the pattern because it changes the way they see themselves. Addicts often refer to themselves as having 'addictive personalities', believing themselves to be more conducive to addictive behaviour than other people. This is not necessarily the case. It may just be that they have come to see themselves that way, perhaps through re-peated failures to give up, or the tendency to replace one addiction with another. They forget that they have not al-ways been so, that when they were children they didn't compulsively overeat or go on rash spending sprees with a credit card.

The meditation exercises of dharana and dhyana (*see* Chapter Eight) are particularly helpful for stripping away the ideas about yourself that you have built up over the years. Discovering the core of your being is sometimes referred to as finding the 'inner child', the person you started out as. This idea is very useful for those trying to break out of destructive adult habits. The added benefit is that not only will you feel physically healthier as a result, you will feel mentally stronger, and able to resist the pat-terns of addiction in the future.

A hatha asana that smokers often find very beneficial is

the fish pose (*see* Chapter Four), which makes them very aware of their lungs. The breathing exercises help to develop awareness too, and are a joy when you feel your lung capacity increase as a result of having given up.

Yoga and youthfulness

Forget face-creams and plastic surgery, wonderfoods and vitamins; yoga is your best bet in the quest for eternal youth.

Yoga practice will not only ease up the joints and muscles that time can tighten, it actually *slows* down the ageing process. This may sound miraculous, if not a little ludicrous, until you consider that chronological time and organic time do not run parallel. For instance, 40 may seem relatively young to us, who can anticipate a lifespan of nearly twice that, but to a medieval person, 40 was old indeed. By 40, one had to have lived one's life whereas nowadays we enter the fourth decade feeling as if we are simply embarking upon a new stage of our progress. This longevity is not simply down to advances in diet in medicine. It is also, in part, due to the resultant expectation of long life. We are simply not attuned to the idea of dying in middle-age, so do not 'wind down' towards it.

This increase in life-expectancy can be enhanced by yogic practice, primarily because it induces serenity, which is the very antithesis of what ages us, organically, most quickly – stress.

Worry is another cause of premature ageing, and can lead to illness and early death. The ancient yogis were well versed in the art of holding their anxieties at arm's length in order to see better how to neutralize them. They knew that this was a better system than attempting to ingest problems whole, and that it kept them resistant to disease. In the late twentieth century we are beginning to catch up a little on their wisdom, as we discover such concepts as the 'cancer personality', a series of personality traits including anxiety, which are thought to increase their possessors' vulnerability to cancers. Ailments as various as cystitis, migraines and recurrent 'flu can have their root in unresolved conflict.

Freedom from anxiety will also prevent the development of that inevitable, physical manifestation of worry: frown lines.

Yoga also leads to self-knowledge and a will to live with integrity. In other words, to be true to yourself. This does not simply mean *not* living a lie. It also means listening to yourself and having the courage to be who you are. People who can do this retain a quality of youthfulness that others, who maybe feel that they compromise themselves by going against their nature, find so elusive. This youthfulness stems from the fact that they are not troubled by the many conflicts that arise from pretending to be who we are not, whether that be in matters of taste, political or religious belief, or choice of friends and lifestyle.

Think of Cliff Richard, renowned for his 'Peter Pan' agelessness. Of course, you may say that his wealth has cushioned him from some of life's harder knocks, but remember that wealth goes a very little way to resolving dilemmas. Indeed, history is rich in examples of 'poor little rich kids' made wretched by their fortunes. No, Cliff Richard's secret is that he lives with integrity. He is honest about the person he is, undaunted by the currently unfashionable nature of his Christian beliefs, or the critics of his music. Whether you are a fan or not, you cannot deny that he is in on the biggest anti-ageing secret of them all: self-belief.

On a physical level, yoga exercises improve muscle tone and circulation. This latter will give your skin more elasticity, resulting in a more youthful complexion. More flexible muscles will put a spring in your step, another attribute of youth.

Finally, the increased confidence that yoga engenders will effectively put you at the controls of your own life. Once you truly *feel* that you are the person in charge of your destiny, long life is sure to follow. After all, the decision is yours.

Chapter Four

The Hatha Postures
(Asanas)

The following chapter is a how-to-do guide for each hatha posture, called an asana. Do not expect to be able to do them all at the first attempt, and remember that it is more important to be able to do a few of them well, than all of them badly. Pay particular attention to the warm-up and relaxation exercise (corpse posture) as these *must* be included in your daily sessions. After all, you would not embark on an aerobics session without first allowing yourself a few minutes preparation and no more should you neglect this part of a yoga session. Even though it seems the gentlest of exercises, you are about to give your muscles a serious work-out.

Remember too that it is important to balance each asana with its symmetrical opposite. For every forward stretch, do a backward one, a stretch to the left followed by a stretch to the right. This ensures that every muscle you flex is given the opportunity to relax.

If you suffer from high blood pressure, have any heart problems, or are menstruating, omit the inverted postures, such as the shoulder and head stands. If you are at all unsure about the wisdom of attempting anything vis-a-vis your state of health it is imperative that you seek the advice of your doctor. In almost all cases, however, doctors will be delighted by your initiative.

Do not be discouraged by any ideas that yoga is for slim people only. Being overweight may make some of the exercises difficult but do not lose heart; in time you will gradually master them. Many overweight people who have tried yoga have found it to be a gateway to other exercises as regular practise increases their flexibility and muscular strength. The added bonus is that yoga can help people overcome weight problems. Not only does it tone muscles, leading to a more slender physique, it can lead you to a more balanced and healthy approach to diet. Those who have lived a very sedentary lifestyle will also find that yoga rejuvenates them and increases their appetite for physical exercise.

The first time you try some of these asanas you may find them uncomfortable. If so, do not torture yourself by holding them for any length of time. Hard as it may be to believe, these postures will one day come to seem very comfortable! Keep this book handy at all times and study the postures over and over again to ensure that you are doing them correctly. If you are unsure, look for a teacher to guide you on the finer points and use this book as a backup for yoga practice at home.

Diaphragm breathing

To fully benefit from the following exercises it is essential to breathe properly. We start out in life breathing correctly, yet most of us, by the time we reach adulthood, wind up breathing the wrong way, using only the upper body. Our idea of a good deep breath is to puff out the chest and squeeze in the tummy, like a sergeant major standing to attention, when in fact our chests should stay where they are. The action should be taking place a good deal further down, at the diaphragm.

The diaphragm is the long flat muscle situated at the bottom of your lungs. To locate it, place your hand on your stomach, just below your ribs, and cough. You will feel a muscle tremble underneath your hand: this is your diaphragm. Now, keeping your hand where it is, repeat that coughing action slowly, but this time without restricting the flow of air from your throat, which you do when you cough. You will feel that a column of air is being pushed up through your body and that your diaphragm is contracting as it rises in accordance. Inhale deeply and you will feel the diaphragm expand as it lowers. Try holding a dictionary, or similar weight object, above your head. As you breathe you will be able to feel the diaphragm rising and falling. Focus on breathing using this muscle alone, remembering to keep your chest in and your shoulders down.

Opera singers and wind instrument musicians are well aware of the power of diaphragm breathing. Without it they would not be able to produce long, pure notes with their voices or control the volume and purity of sound from, for example, a clarinet. Short, weak breaths produce only warbling songs and ghastly clarinet squeaks! Next time you watch Pavarotti perform, note how his chest does not rise or fall with his voice; the air that is powering his voice is being pumped up by his diaphragm.

Breathing in this way stimulates the solar plexus, the network of nerves that supply the abdominal area which is situated in what we refer to as the 'pit of the stomach'. A good supply of oxygen to this area will keep the inner organs, such as the kidneys and pancreas, functioning efficiently, which is clearly good for all-over health. It is here also that the Manipura chakra is situated. According to yogic wisdom, it is from here that the life-force stems, the 'inner fire' that pushes us forward in life. Think of it as a fire that needs air to burn brightly. Shallow breathing will leave it sputtering and weak. It is this area that we refer to when we talk about a 'gut feeling', an instinct so strong that we feel it as opposed to just thinking it, and therefore tend to trust it more. Good yogic breathing will help to sharpen up your instincts too.

Diaphragm breathing requires a lot of practise in order

to be able to do it without thinking. You do not need to restrict your practise of it to yoga sessions. Try doing it at odd moments throughout the day, until it becomes second nature.

Mindfulness

Breathing correctly can bring about a state of 'mind-fulness'. Mindfulness is the mindstate wherein we become very aware of our own self and the world around us. When we talk about 'living in the moment' we are referring to instances where we sink into an experience, and live it fully. This is not to be confused with the notion of recklessness, where caution and responsibility is thrown to the wind, but rather a moment when every channel of receptivity, every sense, is fully alert, and we are alive to the richness inherent in even the most mundane moment. In his poem *Stopping By Woods On A Snowy Evening,* the American poet Robert Frost describes just such a moment on a dark and cold night when he interrupts a long journey, and his cycle of conscious thought, to gaze at the forest: *'The only sound's the sweep/Of easy wind and downy flake./The woods are lovely dark and deep.'* The reader can almost feel the stillness and serenity in which the poet basks before pulling himself back to the task in hand: *'But I have promises to keep/And miles to go before I sleep.'*

The teachings of Zen Buddhism advocate the same principle of alertness to the immediate. Only by learning to surrender ourselves, if only once in a while, to the here and now can we appreciate the beauty of the universe and truly live. Next time you are washing the dishes try a little Zen. Clear your mind of all stray thoughts and tune into the moment by concentrating on what you are doing to the exclusion of all else. Really feel the temperature of the water, focus on the soapy bubbles, the action of your hands and how the dirt lifts from the dishes. Listen fully to the scrape of cutlery against the side of the basin. When you come out of your reverie, you will feel refreshed and probably discover that you have done a spanking job on those dishes. And you never know, you may even come to find the experience of washing-up quite a pleasurable and relaxing one.

This is the state of mindfulness to which yogic teachings refer, and which can greatly enhance the effectiveness of the hatha postures. When doing your daily yoga session, try to do them in the Zen manner described above, focusing on how your body feels and what you are doing. Eventually this habit of tuning in to what you are doing will filter into your daily life, greatly enriching it.

Sitting, standing and lying positions

Lay out your blanket or mat, ensure that you are wearing nothing that is constricting, and begin by sitting down cross-legged. If this is too much of a strain on your thighs then prop up each knee with a cushion. Feeling uncomfortable will only sabotage your chances of relaxing. If this is still a strain, stretch your legs out in front of your body, about shoulders' width apart, with knees bent. You might want the further support of a folded-up blanket to sit on. Try not to be disheartened by difficulties as your aches and pains will begin to ease up.

Make sure that your weight is not resting on the base of your spine but on your pelvic bone. The shape of your abdomen will tell you if you are sitting correctly as it should be long and straight, not squashed and curved inwards. Straighten your back, lift your head and relax your shoulders. Imagine that there is a piece of string attached to the crown of your head, lifting it slightly towards the ceiling, but not so much that your spine 'locks' – you are not on military parade. Place your hands, palms upward, lightly upon your knees. Take a deep breath and exhale slowly. As you breathe try to focus on your body and how it feels. Let your shoulders rise and fall naturally with your breath.

Now imagine that each intake of breath as clean, white light and each outward breath as grey and smoky. Think of the white light as forcing out the tensions and niggles that have gathered inside you during the day; breathe out that meeting, that traffic jam, that overdraft, and breathe in a mountain stream.

Allow yourself as long as you need to thoroughly focus on what you are doing, where you are and how your body feels. This is your very own time; allow yourself to sink into it. The world can wait.

Once you are relaxed, give your arms a little stretch and slowly stand up. You are about to do the 'mountain' (*tadasana*). This is a very simple asana that is surprisingly beneficial. In fact, the first time you try it you will become acutely aware of how rarely you really stand erect. You will feel years of slouching simply fall from your shoulders.

The mountain (tadasana)
Begin by waking up your feet. Stand on tip toe a couple of times, then return them flat to the floor. Give your toes a good wriggle to get the blood moving and then stand with your feet together and your spine straight. Keep your knees loose by concentrating on lifting the muscles above them. Check that your abdomen is straight, not bulging out or curving in, and tuck in your buttocks. Let your hands, palms in, rest on the sides of your thighs.

Take a deep breath and relax your shoulders and open your chest. Remember the string between the crown of your head and the ceiling, and allow your facial muscles to relax. Breathe naturally and feel how your body maintains its balance, feel the space around you and the floor under your feet. This is best done with your eyes closed. You will become aware of every muscle and tendon, and this awareness will gradually filter into your general con-

The mountain

sciousness resulting in a wonderfully improved posture. Standing and walking erect will not only make you appear slimmer and more dynamic, it will also improve your all-over health by allowing you to breathe more efficiently.

The warm-up

1 Standing in the tadasana keeping your face forward. Take a deep breath and as you exhale, slowly tilt your head to the left, your ear towards your shoulder. As you breathe in, raise your head back into the centre and tilt to the right upon the exhale. Repeat six times for each side. Concentrate on keeping these movements fluid and even. Sudden jerks could prove very painful.

Now lower your chin to your chest upon the exhale, raising it to the forward position on the inhale. Repeat three times, then lower your head backwards, again as you breathe out, and return to

45

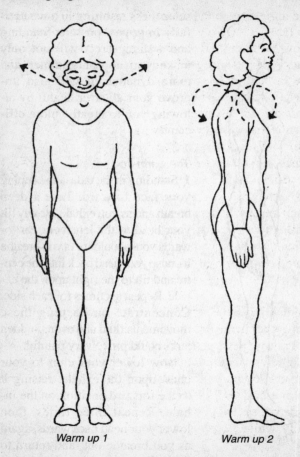

Warm up 1   Warm up 2

the upright upon the inhale. Try not to bend your head so far back that you squeeze your neck muscles.

2 Now lift both your shoulders up and back in a gentle backward rotation, as if you were describing a small circle in the air. Try to keep these circles as perfect as possible. Do this five times then repeat this exercise in a forward motion, again five times.

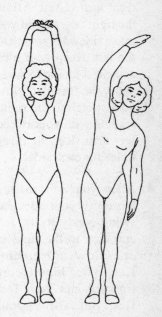

Both 1 and 2 are great little exercises for releasing neck and shoulder tension throughout the day, something those who work over computers or typewriters are particularly prone to.

3a Remaining in the tadasana, raise your hands up above your head. Keep your arms parallel and intertwine your fingers so that your hands form a bridge. Still facing forward, stretch your arms fully while keeping your

Warm up 3a and b

47

feet flat on the ground. This will give your spine a good stretch.

3b Now return your left arm to your side, resting it palm downward on the side of your left thigh, keeping your right arm raised. Allow the right arm to lead you into a sideways stretch to the left. Keep your hips and chest facing forward and your feet flat. Now do a stretch to the right, leading with your raised left arm. Repeat three times for each side.

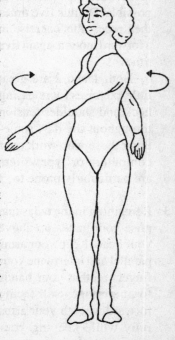

4 Allow your arms to hang loosely by your sides and swing gently to the left and then to the right in one slow movement. Keep your hips facing forward and your feet flat, but allow your shoulders and head to move with the swing. Repeat three times.

Warm up 4

5 Now for a back stretch. Fold your arms behind your back, holding each elbow with the opposite hand. If this is too much of a strain, place both hands on the small of the back. Holding firmly with your hands, tuck in your buttocks, push your hips out and your head and shoulders back, so that your body forms a backward curve. Your weight should be centred on your heels. At first, you may find this uncomfortably precarious, in which case you may want to hold onto the back of a chair to steady yourself. Do not, however, transfer any of your weight from your heels as you may topple over backwards.

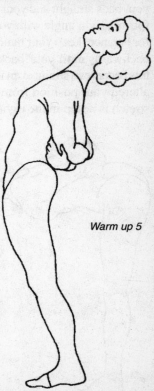

Warm up 5

6 For the forward stretch, keep your arms folded behind you or resting on the small of your back, and lean forwards towards the ground. Bend from the hips, keeping your back straight and your chin forward, until your torso forms a right angle with your legs. If you need the chair for balance, keep your hands on the back and gently step backwards until your back is straight. Stop the instant this becomes a strain, even if you feel that you have barely altered your position from the upright. Even the tiniest stretch is a step in the right direction.

Warm up 6

7 Now for the legs. This exercise often requires the support of a chair back, which should be positioned by your right side. Facing forward, raise your right arm or hold the chair back, and bend your left leg so that your heel reaches your right buttock. Grip your ankle with your left hand and hold. Ideally the left knee should be facing downwards. This is a stretch that sprinters often do before a race, and is excellent for cooling down as well. Hold for a short period, or until it becomes uncomfortable, then repeat for the opposite leg.

8 Repeat step 3. Then give your legs a gentle shake and your arms a gentle shake.

Warm up 7

The cat

This asana evolved from studying the movements of cats as they lazily stretch after a nap, or interrupt a walk to take give their legs an energizing flex, and it helps to think of the way a cat would move when mastering this movement. It is also a great way of waking up your whole body as it boosts the circulation.

Kneel on all fours with your hands a shoulders' width apart and your knees the same distance apart as your hands. Keep your arms straight throughout the entire exercise if you can. Take a deep breath and, as you exhale, move your chine down to your chest so that you are looking down towards your abdomen. Arch your back, making your shoulders round and keeping your buttocks down. Your spine should now be stretched into a very gentle C-shape.

The cat (position 1)

As you inhale, hollow your back into a concave position and lift your head, curving your neck and shoulders upwards. Your spine should now form a shallow inverted C-shape. Repeat these two positions five to ten times, concentrating on creating a slow fluid movement. Think slow langourous cat, not bucking bronco, throughout!

The cat (position 2)

The cat (advanced)

From the starting position for the cat, take a deep breath, exhale and arch your back. This time, however, take your right knee and bring it forward towards your forehead. Bring your forehead down to meet it.

On the inhale, hollow your back as before, with your head curved up, and push your right leg back and up as far as you can go. Do not kick your leg back. Return to the

53

The cat (advanced) positions 1 and 2

starting position and repeat for the left leg. Repeat three to four times each, or until you feel tired. This is a very vigorous asana so it requires quite a lot of physical strength to keep the movement fluid and controlled.

The canoe

This is a good exercise for toning the abdominal muscles, as well as the spine. Begin by lying on your front with your arms stretched out in front of you, your legs stretched out behind with the backs of the feet making contact with the floor, and your chin resting on the floor. Keep your hands and feet about a shoulder's-width apart.

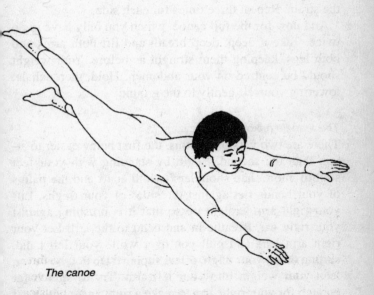

The canoe

Take a deep breath and as you inhale, lift your right leg and your left arm and stretch them both out straight. Allow your head to move upwards but not so far as to stretch your neck. Try to keep your left hip and right shoulder in contact with the floor. As you exhale, slowly lower your arm and leg to the floor. Inhale and do the same wit the left leg and right arm. Do not hold the position for so long that you cannot help but collapse under the strain. Repeat three times for each side.

And now for the full canoe, which you only have to do twice. Take a deep, deep breath and lift both arms and both legs, keeping them straight as before. Your weight should be centred on your abdomen. Hold, then exhale, lowering yourself gently to the ground.

*The triangle (*trikonasana*)*

There are two versions of this, the first being easier to attain than the second. Begin by standing with your feet slightly more than shoulders'-width apart and the palms of your hands flat against the sides of your thighs. Lift your right arm straight up so that it is brushing against your right ear. Breathe in and bend to the left. Let your right arm lead and pull you over while your left hand, sliding down your thigh, offers support. Do not, however, lean your weight into your left arm. Try to stretch far enough for your right arm to make a right angle with your legs and keep your face and hips facing forward.

The triangle

This not only stretches your spine, it also stretches the muscles of your chest and waist too. As you exhale, move slowly back into the standing position and repeat for the other side. Repeat three times each way.

The second triangle requires you to stretch without the assistance of the pulling arm. Begin by standing upright and stretch out your arms to either side so that they are parallel with the floor. Extend the right foot to the right hand side and, as you exhale, bend over towards the right so that your right hand slides down your thigh in the direction of the ankle. There should be no forward inclination of the body at this time. As the bending action takes place, your left arm should be lifted upright with the palm of the hand facing forward. Your right leg, right arm and torso should now form a triangle. This stretch should be maintained for the minimum of a minute. Try to extend the stretch as you exhale. You will find that if you rest for a second and then try again to extend, your body will give a little more. As you inhale, return slowly to an upright position, and repeat the stretch to the left upon the inhale. Repeat three times for each side.

To keep the movement fluid, think of your spine as a piece of elastic being stretched lengthwise as well as sideways. But take care not to ping back too abruptly. When done properly, this is a very calming exercise, partly because it requires such intense concentration. It is also very beneficial in speeding up the expulsion of toxins from the body as it tones the pancreas and kidneys, helping them to operate more efficiently.

The tree (vrksasasana)

This is a classic meditative, or praying, pose. You sometimes see drawings and photographs of Hindus praying in this one-legged posture, as it is an excellent way of focusing the mind. Mastery of it will make you feel like a real Yogi! Its other benefits include improved balance and posture, and makes your aware of the importance of evenly distributing your body weight between toes and heels. You might like to use the chair for support initially as good balance is required.

Begin in the tadasana, focusing your eyes on a spot in front of you. Re-

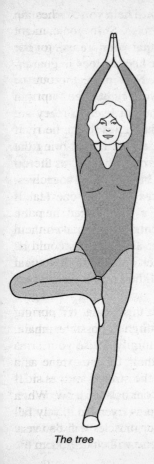

The tree

member to keep focusing as this will help you to maintain your balance throughout the exercise. Shift your weight onto your right foot. Make sure that your are using your entire foot, as balancing on your heel or toes is guaranteed to have your toppling over. Now place the sole of your left foot onto the inside of your right knee. You can use your hands to help. Allow the left knee to relax – it does not need to stick out at right angles to the body. If you need to hold onto the chair, do so. If not, bring the palms of your hands together at chest height, as if you were about to pray. Take a deep breath, close your eyes, and feel how your body balances itself on one leg. It might help to actually think of a tree, rooted into the earth. Many people find this mental image makes them feel surprisingly secure. Hold for as long as is comfortable and then lift your left foot back onto the floor. Repeat the process for the other leg, and then repeat three times for each side.

Once that you feel secure with this asana, try placing your left foot as high up on your thigh as possible. Again, allow the knee to slope down naturally. Raise your arms above your head, stretched to their fullest extent, and bring the palms together. Enjoy the stretch and relax. If you think too much about losing your balance it becomes a self-fulfilling prophecy. Also, if you worry about it, your fall will be all the more painful as your muscles will be tense, and the soothing effect of the exercise will elude you.

*The cobra (*bhujangasana*)*

'Bhujanga' means serpent and the asana that bears its name resembles that of a cobra rearing up to strike. It is a posture that stretches the chest and abdomen. Do not bend so far back that you cannot prevent yourself from collapsing forward; this should be an easy, natural movement.

Begin by lying face downwards on the floor with your hands under your shoulders and your elbows bent. As if you were about to do a press-up except that your feet are flat, not tucked in at the toes. Keep your feet together throughout the exercise. Inhale deeply and, making sure that your hips and legs remain in contact with the floor, slowly lift up your head and upper body, so that your back is curved, your chin facing the ceiling and your arms straight. Do not allow your shoulders to hunch up towards your ears.

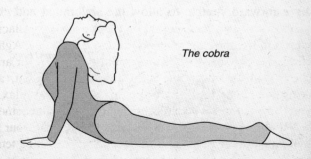

The cobra

Hold for a short period, focusing your attention on the small of your back and the proud sinuous curve of your chest and neck. Slowly relax, lowering your torso, then your chin, nose and forehead, to the floor. To increase the spinal stretch, keep the arms close by your side and move the palms closer together on the floor. To reduce the stretch, vice versa, and allow the elbows to bend.

This exercise helps to tone the abdomen and buttocks, and speed up the elimination of fat from the waist and hips. It is particularly beneficial to women as it increases the blood supply to internal organs including the ovaries and uterus and can help to regulate the menstrual cycle. It is also useful in combating digestive and kidney problems.

The forward bend (paschimotanasana*)*
A backward stretch should always be followed, or preceded, by a forward stretch, to allow the abdominal and chest

The forward bend

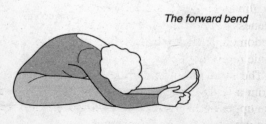

muscles to contract. The forward bend stretches the entire back of the body, from the neck to the knees, and requires a fair amount of suppleness. However, as always, you are the judge of how much of a stretch you can cope with. In Sanskrit, the word 'Paschima' means West. Traditionally, you would face the East for all your yogic exercises, and therefore your body would be getting stretched on its Western side.

Sit with your legs stretched out in front of you, knees very straight, and feet together. Inhale and stretch your arms above your head. Exhale very slowly and smoothly bend forward from the hips (not the waist) to grasp your toes. If, at first, this seems difficult, reach for your ankles, calves or knees. It is important that your legs remain straight. Continue to bend forward and down, aiming to touch your knees with your forehead. Hold for at least ten seconds and observe your breath. Release the hold and very slowly unroll your spine, returning to a sitting position.

The forward bend slows the respiratory rate to produce a calm and relaxed state of mind. It also increases the suppleness of the spine and improves blood circulation in the abdomen, improving digestion and the health of the female reproductive organs.

The more supple may like to begin the forward bend from a lying down position. From here, the aim is to lift the upper body, unaided and without jerking, while keeping your legs flat on the ground.

The bow (dhanurasana)

This posture resembles a drawn bow and it helps when performing it to think on the curved tautness of the wood. To begin, lie flat on the floor with your arms by your sides and your legs flat. Keeping your thighs on the floor, raise your knees so that they touch the buttocks and reach for your ankles with your hands. Take a deep breath and as you exhale, pull with your hands to lift your legs as high as possible, while arching the front of your body and raising your chin up towards the ceiling. Remember the slow curve of the bow and try not to do this movement in a single, sudden jerk. Keep your toes pointed away from your body and your heels pointed towards your head. Your weight should be centred on your abdomen. Try to keep

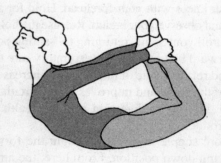

The bow

your legs together but if this is too much of a strain, you may need to begin with your legs apart. Hold this pose and the outward breath and then, as you inhale, relax into your original position.

This stretch is great for the spine, making it more flexible and strong. Because it stretches the whole front of the body, it also has a spectacular effect on posture as it loosens up the accumulated tensions created by stooped shoulders and a slouched stance. The energizing effect this has will make you want to walk tall. The bow also tones inner organs and is especially good for liver and kidney health and promoting efficient digestion.

The bridge (satu bhandasana)
This posture is very soothing and give the abdomen and thighs a really good stretch. Begin by lying on your back with your arms by your side and your legs slightly apart.

The bridge

Bend your knees and bring your heels in beside your buttocks. Support your hips with your hands and, as you take a deep inward breath, lift your torso and thighs till they form a line. Now move your hands to support your lower back, remembering to play the fingers for maximum support. Lift your spine between you shoulder blades and relax your facial muscles. When you are comfortable and feel that the pose is stable, remove your hands and lay your arms our flat, linking the fingers underneath your body.

For an extra stretch, incline your body as far as it will go to the right without lifting your shoulders from the floor. Return slowly to the centre and then incline towards the left. To make the bridge a little bigger, pressure can be exerted by bracing the arms and feet. Try not to squeeze your shoulder with your upper arms when doing this. Hold this position for at least a minute and then allow yourself to sink slowly back onto the floor.

The wheel (chakrasana) (16)

A more advanced version of the bridge is the wheel, which you may also recognise as the 'crab'. This posture gives the whole frontal body a good stretch but should not be attempted until you are comfortable with the previous exercise.

As before, begin by lying on your back, with your knees bent and your feet flat on the floor. Now place your hands,

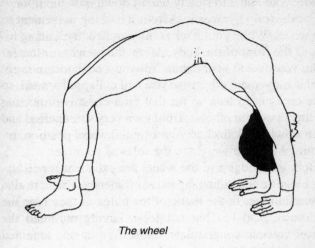

The wheel

palms downward, on either side of your head with the fingertips facing your feet. Lift your buttocks slightly and feel your weight being borne equally by your hands and feet. Take a deep breath and, as you inhale, raise your torso till your back is fully arched. Tuck your head in so that you face the floor. Hold this pose for only a few seconds at first. It is a very dynamic and athletic stance and is more tiring than it looks. Do not let yourself become so exhausted that you crash back onto the floor. Instead, when you are ready to come down, bring your head back so that it faces out the way, and gently stretch your neck.

Allow your spine to slowly uncurl down onto the floor.

For the truly gymnastic there is a rocking movement to the wheel. While your back is fully arched, try leaning towards the front of the body. Allow the weight to transfer from your feet to your hands. You must be in total control of this movement otherwise you will collapse forward, so take care not to lean so far that your chest is projecting further than your elbows. Hold for a very short period and then slowly rock back to your original wheel position, returning half your weight to the soles of your feet.

Both the bridge and the wheel are excellent for reducing bloating and aiding digestive efficiency. They are also powerful allies in the battle of the bulge as they tone the abdomen. And last but not least, having mastered the wheel you can congratulate yourself on having regained some of your childhood suppleness.

To relax your abdomen after these exercises, lie on your back and bring your knees up to your chest. Hold the knees lightly with your hands and enjoy the sensation of those hard-working muscles contracting.

The spinal twist (matsyendrasana)

The last two exercises are of enormous benefit to preventing back trouble as they strengthen and flex the spine. This next asana, and its variations, will also strengthen the back. Lower back twinges will gradually diminish thanks, in great part, to this particular posture, so long as it is done correctly. Throughout this exercise concentrate on relaxing and moving slowly and fluidly. After all, sudden jerks can be extremely painful, as anyone who has ever done given their back 'a nasty turn' will tell you. The subsequent misery could put you off yoga for a long time.

Begin by sitting on the floor with your legs in front of you. The backs of your heels should be on the floor with your toes facing up the way while your back is straight. As with the sitting position at the very beginning, do not sit up too stiffly but as if the crown of your head were being pulled slightly in the direction of the ceiling. Bend the right leg and lift it over the right leg at the knee. Use your left hand to support your upper body by placing it behind you, palm down, at the centre of your spine. Avoid putting

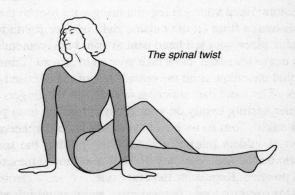

The spinal twist

any weight on this hand if you can. Place your right hand
on the floor beside your left thigh. Take a deep breath and,
as you exhale, twist your upper body to the left, leading
with your head, but letting your shoulders do the pulling
work. Keep your buttocks and legs firmly on the ground.
Try to twist a little further round upon the second exhale.
Hold for perhaps a minute then slowly resume your starting position. Repeat this movement for the other side. It is
important to relax during this movement in order to keep
it fluid, and to make the most of this asana's gift for promoting a sense of psychological balance.

Once you have learnt the spinal twist you are ready to
attempt it with the legs bent. Begin as before, then bend
your right leg in and under so that the foot is making contact with the groin area. Keep the whole leg on the floor if
possible. Bend your left leg and bring your foot so that it
rests on the floor on the outside right of your right knee.
Again, place your left hand behind your back, remembering not to lean on it. Now take your right arm and crook it
so that the elbow is on the outside left of the upraised left
knee. The hand can either be raised with the fingers together, resting lightly on your waist or holding onto your
left ankle. Turn to look over your left shoulder, keeping
your shoulders relaxed and avoiding putting too much
strain on the neck muscles. Hold then return to the original position. Repeat for the other side.

This exercise tones the abdomen and is good for internal organs. It is also very beneficial to the nervous system enabling it to function efficiently.

The fish (matsyasana) (2)
This is best performed after the shoulder-stand as it releases any tensions in the shoulders and neck. It also improves circulation, particularly to the head, thereby stimulating the brain and giving the complexion a boost. Anyone prone to bronchial or other lung-related ailments will benefit from the fish as it works the lungs, expanding their capacity.

Begin by lying on your back with your legs straight out in front of you and your feet together. Arch your back, keeping your buttocks firmly on the ground. Use your elbows (with the forearms and palms flat on the floor) to support you. Allow the head to drop back until the crown is in contact with the floor. This will probably require you to slide your elbows away from the body a little. You should now be really feeling the expansion in your chest. Your weight should be distributed between the crown of the head and the buttocks. Once you feel relaxed and confident in this pose you can remove your elbows from their propping position. Bring the palms together at chest level, as if you were praying, and close your eyes and hold. Breathe calmly and naturally. Return to your original position by slowly lowering your arms so that they support you again, untuck your head and roll your spine down to the floor.

The fish

Once your strength increases you might like to try leg-lifting during this movement, as this will give your thighs and abdomen a wonderfully effective toning session. While in the 'praying' position, take a deep breath. As your inhale, raise your right leg a little distance from the floor. The nearer your foot to the ground, the tougher the exercise. Do not let your leg swing up to a 90 degree angle from the floor. Your leg may be a little shaky the first time so do not hold for long. Slowly lower it as you exhale and repeat for the other side.

The rabbit (3)

This is another good exercise for the lungs. In fact, it virtually constitutes an all-over lung work-out. It is so-called because of its resemblance to the postures of a rabbit, though you will obviously be seeking to avoid the sudden bucking motions associated with this creature when it takes fright and runs.

Begin by sitting on your heels with your feet flat on the ground. Lean forward so that your chest makes contact with your thighs, your head is facing forward and your forearms flat on the ground, palms down. Retain this pose and breathe consciously from the diaphragm, noting how

The rabbit

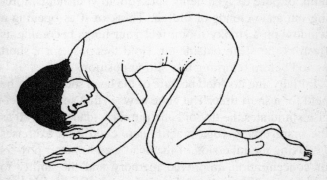

the inhalation of oxygen causes your abdomen to swell, while exhalation causes it to contract. This is a very comforting pose and makes you feel very tucked in and secure. If you feel an unpleasant strain on your thighs, then lift your upper body till you are more comfortable.

Next, sit up so that your hand are palms down in front of your knees and your arms are straight. As before, focus on your abdomen as it responds to inhalation and exhalation. Take several deep breaths before moving on to the next stage, which resembles a rabbit trying to manoeuvre itself into a headstand! Bring your head, crown first, down onto the floor. You might want to move your hands a little further forward to give your head and shoulders some support. Again, listen to your breathing. As you breathe in think of pure oxygen being sucked into your lungs, forcing out stale clouds of old air. Think of it as opening a window on a smoky room; feel your lungs becoming as fresh as the clean outside air. Hold this pose for a short period before returning to a sitting position.

Initially, the inverted posture of the head should only be held for a short time. The good news is that such an exercise stimulates the thyroid and pituitary glands as well as the brain. Many yoga practitioners claim that exercises involving the inversion of the head lead to better powers of concentration, improved memory and the ability to grasp complicated concepts. It is also thought to help ward off senility.

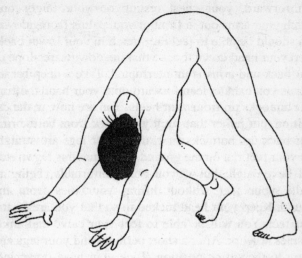

The dog

The dog (7)

Yoga, like many modern fitness regimes, subscribes to the notion that if you 'don't use it, you'll lose it'. So, while it is important to stretch and work the spine, do not forget to include a few asanas that work other areas. The dog is good for toning and strengthening the calves and ankles as well as giving the back and shoulders a good stretch, and should therefore be included in your regular yoga sessions.

Begin as for the rabbit, by sitting on your heels. Now lean forward, your chest resting on your thighs and stretch your arms out in front of you, palms facing down. You should be able to feel the stretch in your lower back. Keep your head down too, so that the downward slope of your back and arms is uninterrupted. Take a deep breath and, as you exhale, lean forward onto your hands, lifting your buttocks up from your heels. You are now in the cat position, but rather than arch your back from here, bring your back up, buttocks first, until your legs are straight and your feet flat on the ground. For some this leg stretch will be enough, but if you are comfortable, being to 'walk' your feet without lifting your toes from the ground. Keep your head tucked in so that you are facing your feet. You will be able to feel your calve and ankle muscles at work. After a short period, bend your legs and return to the sitting position. Tuck your head down into your knees, let your arms relax and enjoy a quiet moment of rest.

The boat (4)

This is almost an inversion of the canoe and would work well with it as it contracts the muscles that the canoe stretches and vice versa. Although it looks as though it requires a great deal of muscular ability, it is in fact more of a balancing act than a feat of strength.

To begin, lie flat on your back with your arms by your

side and your feet together. Take a deep breath and, as you inhale, lift your legs up into the air. They should be at a 45 degree angle to the floor. Inevitably this is going to feel very tiring, so now comes the balancing part. Stretch your arms our in front of you, rather like the arms-out pose adopted by the mummy in Hammer horror films, and then, keeping it straight, lift up your torso till it too is at roughly a 45 degree angle to the floor. Your arms, legs and

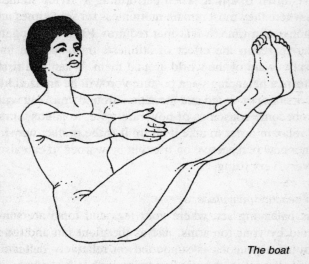

The boat

upper body should now form the shape of an upturned capital 'A'. Try to keep your facial muscles soft and avoid putting too much strain on your neck. To relax, on the exhale lower first your torso, keeping your arms outstretched to take some of the strain. Then lower your legs till your are in the lying down position once again. Repeat three times.

Balancing is a great way of switching off from the world as it requires intense concentration. Performance artists often find that, when performing a 'living statue' act, where they must remain motionless for sometimes up to hours at a time, a feat that requires 100% balance in order to retain the effect of stillness, they become intensely aware of the world around them. When you first perform a balancing yoga posture you will be amazed by the richness of sound and sensation around you. You will also become conscious of how rarely we, as adults, simply relax in order to take it all in. It is the perfect way to gain a new perspective on life, but be warned, it can also be very, very tiring.

The peacock (mayurasana)

This balancing act, where your legs and torso are supported by your forearms, just as the giant fan and long body of a peacock is supported on relatively delicate-looking legs, has an eerie, levitation look to it. And yes, it is as hard as it looks, so for the super-flexible only. If you are comfortable with the wheel then this could be within your grasp. If not, it may need the assistance and advice of a teacher.

Begin by kneeling with you knees spread apart. Your hands should be together, palms downward on the floor, with your wrists facing forward, in the space between your knees. Bend your elbows so that your upper arms, forearms and the floor from three sides of a square. Now lean onto your upper arms and feel your weight centre on your elbows. Only when you feel confident should you begin, on the exhale of breath, to straighten and raise your legs till they are supported by the central axis. Your body should now be parallel to the floor like an undisturbed seesaw. While you are balanced take short breaths but do not hold this position for more than a minute. To relax, breath in, and on the exhale allow your legs to bend and slowly meet the floor. Your weight should shift from the centre slowly, not abruptly.

The peacock

The fixed spot

Concentrating on a fixed spot in your visual field is a time-honoured method for maintaining balance and equilibrium. Ballet-dancers, when performing series of pirouettes, prevent dizziness and disorientation by focusing their gaze on a fixed spot, at eye level, which their eyes seek out at every revolution. This punctuation in the spinning motion is virtually imperceptible to the onlooker, but if you watch closely you will notice that a dancer's head does not rotate at the same speed as the rest of the body. Rather, it will remain facing forward until the body is nearly at the half-revolution stage and then whirl round to the forward facing position once again, at a greater speed than the rest of the body.

Motion sickness is cause by the sense of balance becoming confused. Sailors advocate focusing on the only fixed point observable on a moving ship: the horizon. Similarly, the driver of a car is never the one who suffers from carsickness. This is because his eyes are fixed on the road.

The eagle (12)

This is a gently balancing posture. Begin in the tadasana and focus your gaze on a fixed spot in front of you to help maintain balance. Extend your arms to either side so that they are in alignment, and then bring your left hand in, palm facing, so that your fingertips touch your chin and

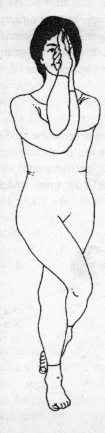

The eagle

your wrist rests on the centre of your breastbone. Now bend your knees and bring the right leg around the left so that your right foot can curl in behind your left ankle. If this seems tricky try bending your knees a little as this move will give you additional flexibility. Your legs should now be in the position of a small child miming that they need to go to the toilet! However, you should not bend over, but keep your spine very straight. Take your extended right arm, bend it at the elbow and slide it under your left elbow. Now curl your right hand round the your left hand so that palms are facing each other, though the left palm will be higher up than the right. Relax your shoulders and feel your chest muscles expand. Hold for a short period, concentrating on that fixed spot, before slowly uncurling, arms first. Repeat this movement for the other side.

81

This asana is very effective for promoting the elasticity of many muscle groups. Many people find that as their physical agility increases so too does their mental agility. So, if you are struggling with an emotional or intellectual problem and feel that your mind is too clouded try practising the eagle. It may help to free up your mind so that you see things more clearly.

The scissors (6)
This asana is so called because it mimics the action of a pair of scissors, where the handle moves in diametric opposition to the blade. If you follow the instructions carefully you will feel an enormous benefit in your lower back as well as in your shoulders and neck. Begin by ly-

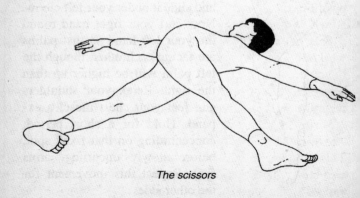

The scissors

ing on your back in a crucifix pose, with your feet together. Consciously make yourself relax and, taking a
deep inward breath, lift your right leg into the air. Think
of your leg as stretching lengthwise as well as upwards.
Once your leg is at right angles to the floor, exhale and
bring your foot down to rest on the floor to the left of your
body, keeping both legs stretched out straight. Your right
hip will rise from the floor but keep your arms and shoulders firmly planted. To assist this movement, turn your
head to the right, just as the handle of a pair of scissors
would move with the action of the corresponding blade.
Relax and hold this posture for at least two minutes. Try
taking another breath and stretching your right leg a fraction further. However, do not jerk – you are not scoring
the winning goal for your country. To come out of this
position, raise your right leg to the 90 degree angle and
slowly lower it to the floor. Repeat for the other side.

This movement is often incorporated into aerobic
workouts as a way of toning the inner thighs. However,
the object here is not to flash from one side to the other,
but to luxuriate in the stretch. Your thighs will tone up
naturally without recourse to such frantic exercise.

The twist (10)
This looks like a halfhearted version of the previous exercise but actually requires an equal dose of concentration
and will give your calves and ankles a good stretch too.

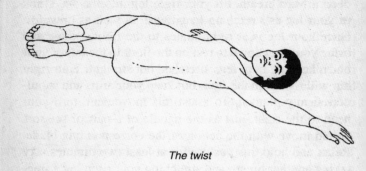

The twist

Lie on your back in the crucifix pose as before, with your feet together and your toes pointing upwards. Take your right heel and lift it so that it rests on top of your left toes. Resist the impulse to raise your head and try to keep your neck and facial muscles soft. Now, upon the exhale, turn your feet so that they point, still one on top of the other, towards the left. As in the scissors posture, turn your head to face in the opposite direction, keeping your arms and shoulders to the floor. Your hips will naturally follow your leg movement. Hold this pose for a minute or two, then point your feet straight upwards once more, and return your right leg to its original position. Repeat the movement to the right, your left foot on top this time, and your head facing left. Repeat three times for each side bur remember to hold the pose each time.

For a bigger stretch, lift both legs in the air, feet together, and twist them down to the right until your knees touch the floor and your thighs are at right angles to the body. You will feel the whole of your spine expand, but remember to keep your shoulders on the floor and your head facing in the opposite direction. Return slowly to the centre and repeat for the other side.

The leg lift (11)

This is a good exercise for people who are trying to lose weight or feel that their stomach muscles have lost some of their tone. It is similar in essence to the stretching exercises performed by athletes limbering up for a training

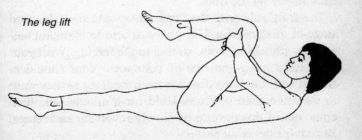

The leg lift

session, and it helps to stretch the hamstrings and is great for relieving, and indeed preventing, stiffness.

Begin by lying on your back with your feet together and your arms by your sides. Bring your right knee up to your chest and pull it a little closer by entwining your fingers behind the knee. Allow your left leg to rise off the floor slightly, but avoid balancing on your tailbone. In the upper body, only your shoulders should be raised from the floor with the majority of your back bearing your bodyweight. This may be as much of a stretch as you want, in which case hold the pose for at least a minute before relaxing into your lying position.

If you want to enhance the stretch then, with your left leg still lifted a couple of inches form the floor, straighten your right leg so that the foot is pointing above and beyond your head. Use both hands, clasped round the ankle, to maintain this pose. Remember, of course, to keep your back firmly on the floor.

The truly rubber-limbed can move onto the advanced stage of this position. Use your left arm to maintain balance by stretching it out parallel to the left leg. With your right hand grasp the tips of your toes. Your shoulders should be at the same distance from the floor as they were in the knee-bend position. Hold for a minute, and then come out of this posture by slowly reversing each stage. Repeat for the other side.

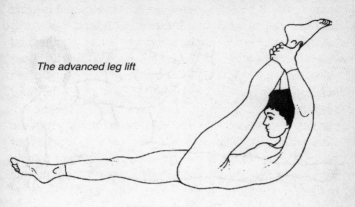

The advanced leg lift

Sideways leg lift (9)

This posture is also referred to, rather confusingly, as the
wheel. It stretches the leg and back muscles and requires
as much balance as it does flexibility. Lie on your left side
resting your head on your left hand. Make sure that your
are lying in a straight line and not bending at the waist or
knees, or inclining forward. Find a spot, at eye level, on
which to focus throughout this exercise, to maintain equilibrium. Once you achieve a stable position take your left
forearm and lay it out flat in front of you. Bend your right
leg up and towards your right ear, and grasp your toes
with your right hand. Keep facing forward, gazing at your
spot. Take a nice deep breath and, as you exhale,

The sideways leg lift

straighten your right leg, maintaining your hold of the toes. Your two legs should now form a right angle. Hold this pose and consciously relax your facial muscles.

This pose is said to represent the wheel of creativity and so should be serene. If your inclination is to frown, then try to smile; you will feel the muscles in your forehead and cheeks begin to relax, and your mood relax with them.

To come out of this pose, slowly bend your leg down and then lift it back onto the other leg. Now turn around slowly and repeat the movement for the other leg.

*Wide side-stretch (*prasarita padottanasana*) (19)*

This is a variant on the dog asana, and will give your backs, hips and legs a powerful stretch. However, if you have back problems do not attempt the full stretch. If you are back problem-free, begin by sitting on your knees with your toes curled so that they are in contact with the floor and your heels are facing upwards. Like an athletes' feet on the starting blocks. Place your hands, palm downward, in front of your knees at a shoulders'-width apart. Leading with your buttocks, and keeping your head tucked down so that you face your feet, raise your back till your arms and legs are straight. Now slowly begin to pace your feet apart to a distance of about four feet. Make sure that you bend from the hips, not the waist, so that your back is straight. Without straining, allow the majority of your weight to focus on your feet, so that your hands are resting quite lightly on the floor. You should be feeling the stretch in the backs of your legs, not in your shoulders.

For an even greater stretch, pace your feet another foot apart and lower the crown of your head to the floor, resting your forearms on the floor beside it and intertwining your fingers at the crown. This is a very advanced stretch and should not be attempted unless you are very supple. Hold this pose for a minute and then lift yourself up, using your hands as well as the muscles in the backs of your legs, to the previous posture.

There are two ways to come out of this posture. You can transfer the weight gently to your hands and allow your knees to bend down towards the floor. Alternatively, shuffle your feet towards the centre, till they are about one to two feet apart. Now shift the weight from your hands to your feet by compressing your abdomen into your back. Your body will naturally rise upwards with the assistance of the upper leg muscles. However, it is imperative that you keep your legs straight as bending the knees will de-

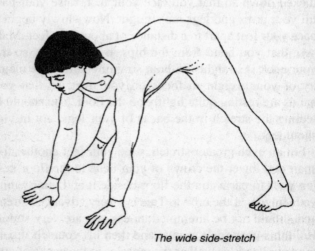

The wide side-stretch

flect some of the strength away from your upper legs and prompt you to jerk yourself upwards to compensate.

If you suffer from any back problems, try doing this posture with a chair. From a standing position pace your feet to around four feet apart and then slowly bend your upper body, from the hips, till they are at a right angle to the floor. Stretch out your arms and hold onto the chair. Remember to keep your weight centred on your feet and feel the stretch in your legs. Relax this hold by walking towards the chair so that your are supported as you move back into a standing position.

The warrior (21)
This is a very empowering pose, reminiscent of the postures struck by ancient warriors about to commence battle. As you would expect, it is an excellent asana for promoting feelings of assertiveness and self-confidence. Begin in the tadasana and raise your arms to chest height, palms facing down, so that the tips of your fingers are touching. Your elbows should be extended straight out on either side. Now pace your feet apart to a distance of four feet and stretch your arms to their fullest extent. Ensure that your toes are pointing forward and your feet are flat on the floor. Your spine should be straight and your shoulders relaxed. Point your right foot out to the right and slowly bend your right knee to the side. Keep your left leg straight with the toes pointing forward. If you can, try to

bend your right knee so that your thigh is at right angles with your lower leg. Take care not to let the right knee overshoot the lower leg as this puts pressure on the ankle and reduces the effectiveness of the stretch as well as jeopardising your balance.

Hold this pose for at least a minute and then return to the central stance. Repeat the movement for the other leg.

The warrior posture

Salute to the sun (surya namaskar)

As the name suggests, the 'salute to the sun' was created as a way of giving thanks for the dawn of another day. The series of movements that follow serve as an excellent warm-up to a yoga session as they rejuvenate and flex every muscle of the body. It can also be a complete session in itself as for every forward movement there is its backward complement, for every left-hand stretch a right-hand one, and so on. Some people base their regular yoga sessions on the Salute to the Sun, incorporating other asanas into the sequence.

It is very important to study and master each movement and to perfect the art of moving from one to the next with fluidity. An observer should believe that you are performing an unbroken ritual or dance rather than a series of stretches punctuated by awkward breaks. Breathe from your diaphragm as this will feed oxygen to every area of your body and keep your energy level constant.

Although these stances are quite safe, they should not be done by pregnant women or those who are menstruating, unless under expert supervision. If you suffer from hypertension (high blood pressure), a hernia, clots in the blood or pain in the lower back, they are not recommended unless on the advice of your doctor. Most doctors will approve of yoga as a form of exercise, especially if you consult a teacher to keep you right, but it is best to check.

1 Begin by facing East, the direction of
the rising sun. Even if this means facing a blank wall, try to fill your mind
with the image of the sun just beginning to appear over the horizon. Even
if it is the end of a busy day, concentrate on that beautifully still, expect-
ant moment just before the sky begins
to lighten. Stand up straight in the
tadasana, with your feet together. Place
your hands, palms together, at chest
level, in the praying posture.

2 Take a deep breath and, as you inhale,
stretch your arms up as far as you can
without taking your feet off the
ground. Lean backwards, pushing out
your pelvis a little, with your palms
facing the ceiling. Allow your head to
tilt backwards so that you are looking
up at your hands. This is a glorious,
celebratory posture. Imagine you are
hailing the first rays of sun and that
the sky is streaked with early morning gold and blue.

3 Take another deep breath and, as you exhale, lower your arms and bend your upper body at the hips, not the waist, and lower it towards the ground. Lower your head too, so that it follows the line of your back and arms. Keep your feet flat on the ground and try to reach your ankles or even the floor at your feet with your fingertips or palms. Do not force this: if you cannot reach the floor, let your hands hold onto the lowest part of the legs they can reach. Don't be disheartened if this is only the knees, as the next time this imaginary sun rises you will be able to stretch a little further.

4 On an inhale, bend both your knees and lift your head so that you face upwards and forwards. Place your hands on either side of your feet to support you. Now gently push your right leg backwards in a long, lunging movement, until your right knee touches the ground. Curl your right toes

under so that they touch the floor and your heel faces upwards and relax your shoulders. Hold for a breath and then bring your right leg back to the knees-bent position and repeat the movement for your left leg. Do these movements gently, remember you are performing a smoothly flowing dance, not violent leg-lunges in an SAS training camp.

5　Keep both hands on the ground, palms down, and raise the head slightly. Lift your hips a little and incline them slightly forward. Taking a deep breath, stretch both legs out together backwards. You can either slide them or step backwards, but don't be tempted to do a big leap unless you are used to lunges, as this can put an unpleasant strain on your upper body. Now raise your body off the ground, supported by your straightened arms, so that your head, back and legs are in alignment. Think of the first of the sun's warmth touching

the crown of your head, and feel the world waking up around you, just as every part of your body is waking up and becoming energised.

6 Exhale and lower your body to the ground. Curl in your toes as in step 4, bend your knees slightly and allow your head to touch the floor. Place each hand, palm downward, under the corresponding shoulder, with your bent el-bows sticking out and up. You should now be in the classic press-up position. Hold this pose for a minute.

7 Take a couple of deep breaths of fresh morning air, and on an exhale, push your knees into the floor and slightly raise your buttocks, so that your stomach and abdomen are not in contact with the floor. Bend your elbows a lit-tle further and bring your chest and chin to the floor.

97

Continue the out-breath and lower your whole body, apart from your stomach and abdomen into the floor, straightening your legs and keeping your toes curled under. Your body is now being supported by the hands at shoulder level and also by the toes. Hold this pose as you take a few deep breaths.

8 On an inhale, straighten your arms so that your back hollows and your chest curves out the way. Tilt your head backwards, facing the sun as it rises into the sky. Your stomach and abdomen will now be in contact with the floor, but keep your toes curled under so that your legs get a good stretch. Hold this pose for a minute and imagine the feel of the sun on your face. You should now be in the cobra position, which is that of a snake rearing up to strike.

9 Take another deep breath and push your whole body upwards, leading with the buttocks. Keep going until your arms and legs

are straight and tuck your head in so that you face your feet. You should now be in an inverted V position. Make sure that your bodyweight is distributed evenly between the curled under toes of your feet and the palms of your hands. Take a deep breath and feel the muscles of your legs and arms come to life.

10 Upon an exhale, push the hips slightly forward and lunge forward with the right leg so that it comes to rest with the knee bent and the right foot flat down between your hands. Remember to do this slowly, even though it is very tempting to make the movement quickly. Breathe in and as you exhale, straighten the right leg, bending the upper body forward and down from the hips. Now bring your left leg in forward so that it stands beside your right. Lift your buttocks high and try to touch your toes, keeping your head tucked down.

11 Inhale and slowly lift the spine, visualizing it as unrolling your vertebrae one at a time. Raise your arms above your head with the palms facing the

ceiling, and lift your head so that your are facing directly into the risen sun. Allow yourself to lean back a little into the stretch, but keep your feet firmly planted on the ground.

12 Lower your arms to your sides and straighten your legs and spine. Keep your head erect and bring the palms of your hands at chest level. You have now returned to the praying position with which you began and your body should be singing with energy and the sun in your mind's eye blazing with warmth.

Salute the sun six times at first, gradually increasing the number of repetitions until you are comfortably doing the routine 24 times. Of course, if you happen to be tired on a certain day, do not force yourself to do so many. Yoga is not about hard and fast rules; the way you feel and your enthusiasm for your practise is much more important than notching up 24 sun salutes a day.

Inverted postures

Inverted postures will initially seem very strange. After all, few of us have done a decent shoulder stand since we were in single figures and are quite unaccustomed to finding ourselves upside down. However, according to ancient yogic wisdom, a child's predilection for upending itself is a healthy instinct as it gives the blood circulation a wonderful boost and help your to feel really in touch with your body. Consider how good it feels, after an exhausting day, to take off your shoes, put your feet up and feel the fatigue drain from your legs. Turning yourself upside down is really just an extension of this.

Please note that these are not suitable exercise for pregnant or menstruating women, or for those suffering from arthritis in the back, shoulders or neck.

The shoulder stand (sarvangasana) (8)

For this posture ensure that your back and neck are protected with a mat or folded blanket, even on a carpeted floor. You might want to give your shoulders the added support of a folded up blanket, as your weight will be resting on this part of your body.

Begin by lying on your back with your arms by your sides, with your palms flat on the floor. Bend your knees and lift them up towards your abdomen. As your lower back begins to lift off the floor, support it with both hands, and lift your knees to chest height. Take a deep breath and as you exhale straighten your legs and body so that they form a right angle with the floor. Avoid lunging by consciously transferring your weight to your shoulders. Your neck should not be taking the weight. Once you have achieved this pose, relax. Breathe normally and enjoy the sensation of your legs and feet being in the air. When you are ready to come down, slowly unroll your body onto the floor, laying your arms out flat to support your weight as it transfers from your shoulders.

The shoulder stand

Pay particular attention to your breathing pattern throughout this exercise. If you find that your breath is quick and shallow then you are tense. Such light breathing starves the muscles of oxygen and is therefore making the exercise counterproductive. If you are tense, abandon this posture meantime and attempt it again when you feel more confident. When performed correctly, the shoulder stand take pressure of the heart and stimulates whole body circulation. The fact that your chin is pressed into the chest is good for the thyroid, stimulating it and helping to iron our problems such as over- or under-activity, thereby helping to even out thyroid-based weight fluctuations.

Once you have mastered the shoulder stand you may want to attempt it without the back support. To do so, repeat the previous instructions but allow your arms to rest lightly on the floor behind you. Remember that your legs and body should form a straight line, like a candle, which is another name for this asana.

Alternatively, you can try resuming the back support (splaying your fingers will broaden the support base) and bending your upraised legs so that the soles of the feet come together.

The plough (halasana)

This asana is so called because it resembles the shape of an old-fashioned Indian plough. It is also sometimes referred to as the wheelbarrow. Begin by lying on your back as before. Supporting the small of your back with both hands, bring your legs up over your head, keeping them as straight as possible. Continue lifting your legs up and over your head until the toes come to rest on the floor behind your head. Only when you are quite comfortable in this pose should you release the hold on your back and place your arms flat on the floor. Initially do not hold this pose for long, perhaps for ten seconds maximum. Once your body becomes accustomed to the plough you may want to hold it for longer.

An extension of the plough is the so called 'choking position'. Obviously, if it makes you feel as if you are actually choking then stop at once. The name derives from the fact that the posture involves your thighs bracing your chin, and looks, to the uninitiated observer, as if you are engaged in a bout of self-throttling.

The plough

To achieve this unique pose, move into the plough as before. Now take a nice deep breath and, as you exhale, bend your legs, bringing your knees down to the floor so that they are as close to your shoulders as possible. Hug the backs of your knees with your arms and gently hold this position. Allow yourself to breathe naturally. To come out of this pose, return slowly to the plough before unrolling back onto the floor. Though at first this will seem like a strange contortion, it will come to feel very soothing and rejuvenating.

The tripod

This rather tricky-looking posture is actually quite simple. It is just a question of confidence and following instructions precisely. If you are unsure, or find it too problematic, then this may be an asana to take to a teacher. Before you begin, take steps to protect your spine and neck by placing a blanket or mat underneath you, even if the floor is already carpeted.

Begin by standing on your hands and knees with the backs of your feet flat on the floor and your head and spine in alignment. Face downwards, and have your hands and knees placed a shoulders'-width apart. Now place the crown of your head on the floor the same distance from each hand as the hands are themselves apart. These three points, the hands and head, must form the three points of an equilateral triangle, otherwise the pos-

The tripod

ture will be imbalanced. Now bend your elbows so that
the upper arms are at right angles to the floor. It is important that your weight is evenly distributed between the
right hand, left hand and head as they are about to take the
full weight of the body.

Carefully and slowly place your right knee onto your
right elbow, making sure it is centred properly so that it
does not slip. If this feels secure, place your left knee on
your left elbow and balance. Caution is essential as you
will end up performing a rather perfunctory forward roll

if you do not achieve sufficient balance. Once you master this position, it is surprisingly comfortable. Concentrate on relaxed breathing. If you find yourself tensing and taking quick, shallow breaths, come out of this posture by lowering each knee in turn and slowly uncurling your torso, head and neck.

The corpse posture (shavasana)

This is the ultimate in relaxation techniques and is an ideal way of cooling down after a yoga session. Begin by lying on your back. Ensure that you are neither too hot nor too cold and that you are as comfortable as you can be. Now visualize yourself lying on a warm beach. Take a

The corpse

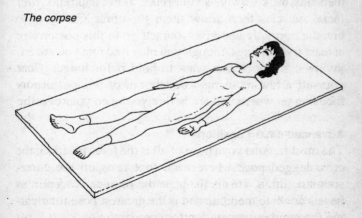

deep breath and feel the sun on your face and let your muscles relax into the soft sand. Allow yourself to breathe normally and enjoy the moment. When you are ready, bring your mind's focus down to your toes. Give them a little wiggle and then flex them. As they relax you will feel a great release of tension. Now move to the soles of your feet and flex and relax them as you did for your toes. Let your heels be heavy in the sand. Remember not to strain, and to perform the exercise slowly. Move up through your legs, tensing and relaxing your knees and then your buttocks. Take your internal gaze to your hands and move up your arms to your shoulders. Lift and flex your shoulders a couple of inches from the ground, and then sink back slowly as your relax. Tense and relax your facial muscles then allow them to soften. Continue to breathe normally and give yourself up to this posture for at least five minutes, though you may find that you are enjoying it so much you want to hold if for longer. Give yourself a few moments to come out of this posture by focusing on where you are before you open your eyes.

Advanced sitting positions

The most famous yoga pose of all is the lotus position; the cross-legged pose where each foot rests on the corresponding thigh. This is the pose the Bhudda is seen in as he sits down to meditate and is the greatest pose for clearing the mind in preparation for contemplation.

   Anyone who has attempted this posture without any prior yoga practice will know only too well that it is a lot harder than it looks, and is one of the prime reasons why yoga tends to be unfairly written off as a weird enthusiasm for tying oneself in knots. However, if the very thought of the lotus makes your legs feel tired, don't worry. There are simpler yoga sitting positions.

The thunderbolt

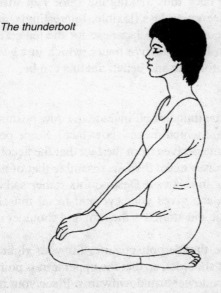

The thunderbolt (vajrasana) (13)

This is the most basic sitting position, and is described at the beginning of this chapter. It is an excellent posture for breathing exercises, as well as for improving digestion and toning the thighs and spine. It is also surprisingly absorbing as it requires concentration to keep the spine and head erect and resist the impulse to slouch backwards. Sitting too erect is also damaging as in so doing, you contract the lower back thus making the spine feel stiff, resulting in its becoming less flexible. Interestingly this is the sitting pose adopted by Japanese for the tea ceremonies which can last up to five hours, which just goes to show how comfortable and beneficial this can be.

The cow-face

Variations on the thunderbolt include the cow posture, or *gomukhanasana*, which means 'cow-face'. Some people say that the name derives from the fact that the accompanying eye exercises make the face resemble that of a cow rolling its eyes in distress! Despite this rather sad little thought, this asana gives your eye and facial muscles a gentle work-out and stretches the arm and shoulder muscles.

Sitting in the thunderbolt posture, lift your right arm over your right shoulder, so that the upper arm is pointing upwards and the lower arm downwards. Place your hand, palm down, on your back, as close to that central bit where you can never quite reach with the sun-cream as possible. Take your left arm and bend it, upper arm down, lower arm up, round your back to meet the right hand. Clasp your fingertips together and feel the stretch, but do not strain your arms by pulling your hands together. Now for that facial. Keeping your head pointing forward, imagine a giant clock (and not a digital one!) in front of your face. Look at the number twelve, which should be above your natural line of vision, without tilting your head upwards or furrowing your brow. Your eye muscles should be doing all the work here. Think of those paintings in haunted house movies where the eyes move but the rest of the face re-

The cow-face

mains motionless; that is the effect you are trying to achieve here. Now move your eyes down and out slightly to one o'clock, then 2 o'clock and so on until you arrive back at twelve. Hold each clock position for a second (count 'one elephant' each time), and continue to breathe normally. When you reach twelve, go round the clock again, but this time in an anticlockwise direction. When you reach twelve again, close your eyes and gently release your arms bringing them round to rest on your knees.

If your eyes feel strained, rub the palms of your hands together to make them warm, and gently cup one over each closed eye. Take a few deep breaths and relax. This eye exercise can be performed at any time and the warm-hand cupping is very effective for reviving eyes that have spent too long straining over text or staring at a VDU screen. It is also wonderfully rejuvenating when your eyes feel tired and gritty.

Learning to move our eyes independently of our heads not only strengthens eye muscles, it gives the neck muscles a rest too. An ophthalmologist called W.H. Bates believed that learning to use our eyes correctly, using the Bates Method, could even make the need for corrective lenses unnecessary. Whether this is so or not, the clock exercise above will certainly develop your awareness of your peripheral vision and help to improve your sense of balance. This latter is because, if we habitually turn our body to look, we risk throwing ourselves off the central axis of our stance; learning to look without moving unnecessarily can prevent this.

The lion

This odd-looking asana is excellent for releasing neck and jaw tension, as well as being rather good fun. Sitting in the thunderbolt, take a deep breath and, as you exhale, stick out your tongue as far as it will go without straining, open your eyes wide and tense the neck and facial muscles. Brace your arms which should be straight with your hands on your knees. Hold this posture for the entire exhalation and then relax, remembering of course, to bring your tongue back in.

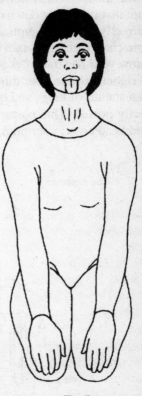

The lion

The Egyptian

If the thunderbolt is not at all comfortable, and you are sure that this is not down to following the instructions incorrectly, try the Egyptian posture. For this you need a firm chair with an upright back, and of sufficient height to allow your feet to be flat on the floor with your lower legs at right angles to your thighs. Think of the ancient Egyptian statues of kings and queens; they are serene and perfectly poised. This posture is identical. Keep your back and head erect; your chin should not jut out further than

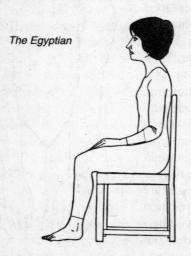

The Egyptian

your forehead, and your abdomen should be long and straight, not squashed. Like the thunderbolt position, this will become enormously comfortable and, after a while, it will come to affect the way you sit outwith your yoga sessions -which is good news for the health of your spine as well as your posture.

Take care when getting in and out of this position. All too often, when we sit down on a chair we fall into it, rather than lower ourselves slowly downwards. The result of the former habit is that we make contact with the chair too heavily, sometimes causing jarring, and, when it is time to get up, we do the opposite, and swing up from the seat, causing uneven and unnecessary strain throughout the whole body. A good way of changing your habits is to practise sitting on an imaginary chair. Notice how you lower yourself down gradually when you know that there is nothing to break your fall, and how you gently tilt your back forward from the hips, keeping it in alignment with the head. As you raise yourself up again, note how your gradually straighten your whole body, legs, head and spine working in harmony. Now try this with a real chair.

The tailor's position
If sitting cross-legged holds no problems for you, then it is simple to advance from here to more demanding yoga postures. The basic cross-legged position, sometimes known as the tailor's position, is actually quite a healthy

posture providing you keep your back straight. Sit with each foot curled slightly under the opposite foreleg, just above the ankle. Straighten your back and place each hand, lightly, on the corresponding knee. Don't use your hands to pull you upright, and ensure that you are not leaning on your tailbone. Relax your knees and avoid jamming your feet under your legs thus causing the unpleasant sensation of 'pins and needles'.

The butterfly

A progression from this cross-legged posture is the but-

The tailor's position

terfly, which will stretch your inner thighs and your hips. This is especially good for anyone keen on horse-riding as it will stretch the muscles used to sit astride a horse's back, thus preventing saddle-soreness.

To achieve the butterfly move from the cross-legged position by stretching your legs out in front of you. Keep them straight, feet together, toes up, and make sure that you are not leaning back onto your tailbone by keeping your back and abdomen straight. Let your arms hang loosely by your sides with your palms on the floor. Now bend your knees away from the body and bring your feet

The butterfly

together so that the soles are flat against each other. Cup your hands around your feet. Concentrate on natural diaphragm breathing and, when you are relaxed, begin to move your knees up and down, like the wings of a butterfly. Keep the movement slow and even and repeat several times. For a final big stretch, gently push your knees down towards the floor. Hold and then relax, cupping your feet once again. When you can move your knees to the floor without using your hands and without difficulty, you are ready for the half-lotus.

The half-lotus

Sit with your legs stretched out in front of you. Take the left ankle and bring the left foot so that the heel is against the groin, between the anus and vulva or scrotum, an area known as the perineum. Take your right foot and lift it across the left leg so that the toes are pointing into the back of the left knee and the heel is touching the groin. Keep your back straight; your weight should be centred on your pelvic floor and your knees touching the ground. Place each hand on the corresponding knee with the palms facing upwards. This is a beautiful, symmetrical pose and you cannot but feel serene when in it. Let your facial muscles soften, close your eyes and hold.

To come out of it, bring your knees up slightly and release your feet, the right foot first. Stretch your legs out in front of you once more and take a deep breath before

The half lotus position

standing up. Always take your time coming out of these postures and vary the legs, leading with your right leg one time, your left leg the next.

The lotus position (padmasana) *(20)*
Named after the beautiful flower that symbolises perfection and creation, this is the ultimate sitting posture and should only be attempted by those thoroughly comfortable with the half-lotus. Many teachers, in fact, insist that this should only be taught on a one-to-one basis.

Begin by sitting on the floor with your legs stretched out, as in the previous exercise. Take your right leg and lift it so the heel rests on the perineum, and the toe reaches high onto the left thigh. Bring the left foot across the right leg so that it rests high on the right thigh, the toes facing outwards, the heel pointing towards the groin. Again, rest both hands on the knees with the palms facing upwards. Hold this pose for a short time and remember, next time, lead with the other leg.

The lotus position

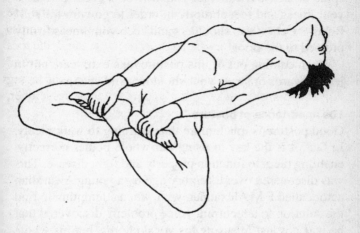

The fish lotus

The fish-lotus

From the lotus position you can move into this version of
the fish asana, which is an entire body stretch but for the
very gymnastic only. Sitting in the lotus position, take
hold of each foot with the opposite hand, i.e. the left hand
holds the right foot and vice versa. Take a deep, deep
breath and, as you inhale, slowly hollow your back, arching it inwards, until the crown of your head comes to rest

121

on the floor behind you. Do not roll backwards with your spine arched outwards as you will be forced to release your knees and feet abruptly in order to go with the roll! Relax the chest and shoulders and keep your knees firmly pressed to the floor.

When coming out of this posture take extra care not to jerk upwards or strain your shoulders and abdomen.

The importance of posture

Good posture is much more than learning to walk nicely. In fact, it is the key to using our whole bodies correctly, enabling them to function properly and fight disease. This was discovered over a century ago by a young Australian actor called F M Alexander, who, when attempting to find the solution to a recurrent voice problem, discovered that he was not just misusing his vocal chords, but his whole body. The technique that he developed to correct this misuse, the Alexander Technique, is not a million miles away from the teachings and methods of yoga.

Alexander found that poor use of the body was not inherent, but learned. The proof of this can be found by observing the movements and postures of infants. For instance, a baby will sit upright if placed on the floor; its spine supple and erect, not curved backwards towards the floor. An unselfconscious infant will bend its knees, keeping its back straight, when lifting a heavy object, and sit and stand upright rather than slouch. So what happens to us that by the time we reach adulthood we have developed a whole host of bad habits that bring about the aches and pains that inevitably make us feel even less inclined to move correctly?

Alexander believed that this is partly brought about by mimicking others. Children are often to be seen studying the movements and attitudes of parents and adults. It is a natural part of a child's learning process, and therefore, if they see their father bending stiffly down to lift a box of books, they will copy that movement. Even as adults we do something similar, unconsciously mimicking the gestures and attitude of someone towards whom we feel sympathetic. This is referred to as mirroring body language, and is a sure sign that someone is listening to you.

Another factor in the development of bad habits is enforced sitting for long periods of time, which we all endured for years at school, leading to all that craning forward and slouching back. Combine this with teenage awkwardness about a developing body and you have a recipe for disaster. Even breaks for PE and playtime fail to rectify this, as much organised sporting activity involves repetitive movements and fails to take into account the need for warming-up, cross-training and relaxation.

Finally, emotional and physical problems can contribute to poor posture. For instance, when we are depressed or sad, we let our shoulders droop and our spine sag. Consider the couple depicted by Picasso in his painting *The Tragedy*, dated 1903. Looking at this sombre work we can see, by the deep blue colours and forlorn expressions, that the couple have suffered a terrible loss or are enduring some appalling crisis. The emotional content is reinforced by their postures; stooped shoulders, arms twisted together, spines curved. Standing beside them is a child, presumably their son, who can be seen copying his father's hunched shoulders' pose.

Physical injury can also throw out our balance, causing us to limp or walk with a bent back, for instance. However, we often tend to continue limping long after it is necessary. We do not do this because we crave extra sympathy but simply because it becomes habitual. Many old people walk in such a way so as to 'compensate' for an old injury that may no longer even be noticeable. This is partly out of a fear that a change in habit will bring about the return of pain, though often the opposite is true. Luckily, as with yoga, there is no such age as 'too old' to begin learning the Alexander Technique. However, the younger you start the easier it will be, and the longer you will have to savour the rewards.

The spine

The spine is the most important bone in the body, influencing the function and health of the nervous system, muscles and internal organs. Yet, for all its importance, we neglect it. Sportspeople and fitness enthusiasts pay enormous attention to their legs, arms, upper body strength, or whatever part of them they think is most important to achieving their ambitions. Far too few truly appreciate the workings and needs of the spine, without which the rest of their endeavours would be pointless. The fact that the spine still manages to retain its strength and flexibility at all when it is neglected is testament of how truly resilient it is.

Allowing the spine to stretch properly and regularly is one of the biggest favours you can do for your body. It will keep the help to keep the vertebrae, and the discs between them, in alignment. Anyone who has ever suffered a slipped disc will tell you just how excruciating the results of poor alignment can be. Not only can it lead to injury, the resultant backaches and discomfort can seriously impinge on your quality of life, as well as your self-confidence.

Each disc has a semi-fluid centre, protected by an outer shell. Think of the vertebrae as individual building blocks, each with a cushion (disc) between them. If the blocks are pushed out of alignment so that they bear down heavily on one or other side of the cushion, the fabric of the cushion will wear away, and the stuffing (semi-fluid centre) begin to squeeze out. The attendant nerves are then subject to pressure, causing pain. Proper stretching exercises keep the vertebrae in their rightful place, thus giving damaged tissue the opportunity to repair itself, thus preventing further damage.

Chapter Five

Ailments – An At-A-Glance Guide to which postures are suited to which ailments

Ageing

Sadly there is no miracle cure for this. Asanas such as the fish and the dog will improve the blood circulation in the face, giving the skin a fresher, more youthful complexion, while regular yoga practise will increase overall suppleness, lending you a more youthful stance.

Altzheimer's disease

Inverted postures, such as the shoulder stand, the dog and the fish-lotus, stimulate the brain, allowing it to function properly. Such postures are believed to help ward off the development of Altzheimer's Disease.

Anxiety

Try a soothing exercise such as the thunderbolt or the serene sideways leg-lift. An asnana that requires total concentration, such as the boat, is also very effective as it lifts your mind out of its anxious state.

Asthma

Breathing problems can be diminished with exercises that increase the lung capacity. Helpful asanas include the fish, the mountain (tadasana) and the rabbit, which gives your lungs a thorough work-out. Pay particular attention to the chapters on yoga breathing as these are very helpful in reducing the symptoms of asthma.

Backache

All yoga exercises help to make the spine more flexible and thereby reduce back problems. Especially recommended asanas include the cat, the dog, the plough and the forward bend. For lower back problems, such as sciatica and lumbago, try the triangle, and for upper back pain try the cow-face. Remember to balance each forward stretch with a backward one.

Bowel problems

Irregular bowel activity is often traceable to the poor functioning of internal organs as well as poor diet. Study the chapter on diet, and look to exercises that tone the abdominal muscles, as these will also tone the internal organs. Try the spinal twist, the wheel and the cobra. The bow is very effective in curing constipation.

Concentration

If you find it difficult to concentrate try an asana that requires you to do just that! Try the eagle and the thunderbolt.

Depression

A great deal of depression is caused by low self-esteem and a basic lack of inner self-confidence. Try the warrior, which is a very empowering posture, and the salute to the sun, which is a very joyous, celebratory sequence of asanas. As you become more flexible and you all-over health improves, you might well find that you are less prone to depression.

Digestive problems

Bloating can be reduced with the bridge and the wheel. If digestive problems persist, consult the chapter about diet. The forward bend aids digestion, as does the bow and the simple, but effective, thunderbolt.

Eye strain

The warm-hand cupping exercise recommended after the cow-face posture is good for soothing tired eyes, while the cow-face exercise itself helps to increase the strength of eye muscles, making the eyes less prone to straining.

Insomnia

Regular yoga sessions will teach you how to relax which will naturally result in improved and healthful sleep. The salute to the sun is a great way to wake up the whole body, if it is tired, and can also help the body to unwind, thus promoting better sleep.

Menstrual irregularity

It is not advisable to attempt any of the inverted positions during menstruation. When you are not having a period, try the plough, which helps to regulate menstrual problems as well as enhance the health of the reproductive organs, and the cobra.

Obesity

Regular yoga practise will promote inner confidence which is often the key to helping someone combat a weight problem. Take careful note of the advice in the chapter on diet; many people find that they naturally tend to healthier eating habits as their body awareness increases. For toning-up, which makes for a more slender physique, try the triangle, which tones leg and abdominal muscles, and increases the elimination of fat from the waistline, as does the cobra and the wheel. The eagle is good for toning up the thighs and is said to be able to eliminate cellulite.

Posture
Again, your posture will naturally improve with regular yoga practise. If you want to really work on your posture, look to asanas that require concentration and balance, such as the tree, the eagle and the tripod.

Thyroid problems
An overactive or underactive thyroid can cause weight to become unstable. Exercise which stimulate the thyroid, thereby promoting its more efficient functioning, include the plough and the tripod.

Toothache
The lion posture eases tension in jaw and neck muscles and can help to alleviate some of the misery of toothache. However, a visit to the dentist is still in order!

Saddle-soreness
To prevent this give the inner thigh muscles and hips a good stretch with the butterfly.

Varicose veins
A shoulder-stand will take the weight off your legs and help to stimulate the blood circulation.

Voice and throat problems

The lion is the one for you. It not only helps to strengthen
the voice-box and can even help to stave off a sore throat
if practised religiously when you feel it coming on.

Chapter Six

Yoga Breathing

The way that we breathe is inextricably linked to our sense of wellbeing and our emotions. When we are frightened or very stressed we start to take very quick, shallow breaths and when we are very relaxed, or asleep, our breathing becomes much slower and deeper. Both these processes are entirely involuntary, caused by the body reacting to signals sent out by the brain. The problem with shallow breathing, while doing us no harm if sustained only for a short period, is that if it affects our general breathing pattern, as it can do when we are constantly under stress, our whole health will suffer. Shallow breathing means that we are using only a fraction of the lungs' capacity, and failing to supply our muscles and organs, via the blood, with sufficient quantities of fresh oxygen. This results in those muscles and organs being unable to function properly.

Try taking a really deep breath right now. Do you feel as if you are taking in a lot more air than usual? And do you suddenly feel more alert than you did a moment ago?

The fact is, lack of oxygen in the blood stream makes us feel tired and prone to headaches. Thus when we feel tired, we yawn. A yawn is the body's way of sucking in more air, just as a thermostat triggers an extra burst of energy in a heating system when the temperature falls below the set level.

Correct breathing can make a huge difference to the way we feel. A few deep breaths can help to ease off a mild case of indigestion. It can wake us up and help us to sleep. It can even help to lower anxiety as focusing on long, slow breaths coerces the mind into slowing itself down too. Recently it has been discovered that learning to play the bagpipes, which requires a great deal of deep breathing to generate enough air, can help to alleviate asthma. This is because the practice of deep breathing increases lung capacity and thereby helps the sufferer to take control of, rather than be controlled by, their breathing patterns.

Pranayama

Yoga breathing is called *pranayama*. 'Prana' means 'breath of life' and 'ayama' means 'interval' so combined it means 'the interruption of breath'. Breath, as well we all know, is the stuff of life. Without it we die. Yogis regard breath as much more than the element oxygen; to them it is the force that connects us with the life-force of the universe. Correct breathing unblocks the channels of energy that run through the body (*see* the Chakras), and balances the negative and positive forces, the masculine and feminine, yin and yang, within us. Please note that all pranayama exercises, unless otherwise stated, should be done with your mouth shut so that you breath through your nose. Before beginning it is best to take a shower, clear your sinuses and rinse out your mouth. As with the asanas, do not undertake these exercises within two hours of a heavy meal, or an hour of a light snack.

Holding the breath

Imagine you are standing at the kerb of a street, cars haring past in both directions. Suddenly you see a football bounce onto the road and, an instant later, a small child run out after it, heedless to the speeding traffic. You hear the squeal of breaks and, in the vital seconds that follow, the world seems to go silent. People in such circumstances have described performing incredible feats of quick thinking and daring without feeling as if it were them actually doing it. 'Something took over', 'I seemed to be watching myself doing it' they might recall as they lie gasping for breath by the roadside, clutching the terrified child. That instant of silence is what is referred to as a 'heart-stopping moment'. In such instances, where fast action is required, we feel as if our heart has literally stopped breathing and some superhuman force has taken control. We become able to do things that normally lie outwith our capabilities. In fact, our heart has not stopped, and no exterior force has moved in on us. The sudden sensation of stillness is caused by our holding our breath, and by doing so, we are enabled to focus our minds totally on the task in hand.

Psychologists have estimated that we use only about 20% of our brain capacity at any given time, simply because we do not know how to fully tap into its resources. The exceptional Albert Einstein is guessed to have utilised as much as 40%, and think how much he achieved in so doing. Of course, holding your breath is not going to turn you into Einstein, but the involuntary action of the body certainly stimulates the brain into given an above-average performance. It enables us to swerve the car out of harm's way at a split-second's notice, police negotiators to talk someone into handing over a weapon in a highly volatile situation and examinees to answer questions correctly in situations on which their futures depend. Without this inbuilt system we would panic, our minds racing hither and thither without settling on a course of action, our bodies become unable to act.

Holding the breath is a means of focusing the mind and, as such, is a very important part of pranayama, especially in training for meditation, which will be dealt with in the following chapter. It cannot be over-stressed that yogic breath holding is not the same as holding your breath in preparation for a underwater dive, or an endurance test.

Under no circumstances should it ever be forced or un-comfortable, and it should be avoided by anyone suffer-ing from hypertension (high blood pressure) or a heart problem.

A simple breath retention exercise to try begins with sitting in the thunderbolt or Egyptian position, with your hands resting lightly on your knees and your eyes closed. Inhale slowly and deeply, but without any sensation of straining. When you have fully inhaled, count to two in your head, and slowly exhale. You should not need to gasp outwards unless you have breathed in too forcefully. Repeat several times, but stop if it becomes unpleasant. Gradually you will be able to build up your breath reten-tion to 60 or even 90 seconds, but avoid feeling as if your must 'better your record'. You are not, repeat *not*, training for the Olympic underwater swimming team.

The alternate nostril breath
This is a classic pranayama technique and helps to restore the yin-yang balance. The fact is, we rarely breathe through both nostrils so this exercise evolved to ensure that we learn how to.

Begin by sitting in one of the sitting asanas as before. Using one of the fingers of your right hand, ideally the third, press the right nostril shut. Breathe in, keeping the right nostril closed, so that your left nostril is forced to do all the work. Now press the left nostril shut as well, using the thumb of your right hand. Count to 16, retaining that breath. Release your right nostril and exhale gently. Now repeat the exercise, beginning with the left nostril closed. Repeat this process five times, but remember to do the exercise calmly and slowly.

This exercise is very good for clearing the sinuses and speeding up the expulsion of phlegm.

The buzzing bee

This is a very soothing exercise, ideal for calming down at the end of a busy, noisy day. Sitting comfortably, allow your facial muscles to relax and shape your lips as if you were about to blow into a flute. Your hands should be resting lightly on your knees. Now close your eyes and imagine yourself sitting on a lawn on a summer's afternoon. Feel the heat of the sun on your face and smell the warm earth and the flowers. Breathe gently and deeply, and then, on an exhale, breathe out through your lips making a steady 'Hmmmm' sound until all your breath has gone. Inhale deeply and repeat several times. This will create a gentle vibration throughout your body and remind you of the sleepy drone of a bumble bee moving from flower to flower. Give yourself a moment or two to 'come to' before opening your eyes.

The bellows breath

Normally, when we breathe in, we do so forcefully, while breathing out is the automatic, passive reaction. A pair of bellows, on the other hand, fills up with air of its own accord and external force must be exerted to pump the air out. The bellows breath mimics this process.

The best way to perform the bellows breath is standing up with your feet pointing outward, your legs slightly apart and your knees bent. Your upper body should be tilted slightly forward, bending from the hips, and your head in alignment with your back, your face looking down. Hold onto the tops of your thighs, palms down, with your elbows bent away from the body. If this reminds you of the postures struck by rosy-cheeked peasants having a jolly good laugh in medieval depictions of country fairs, then well and good. Mimicking the action of a deep laugh will show you exactly how this exercise works. Take a deep breath and then quickly eject the air through your nostrils, as if you were having a long, silent guffaw. You will notice that the air seems to flood back into your lungs without any effort on your part. Try this again. Your inward breath should take longer than your outward breath, but take care to avoid forcing the breath out for longer than is comfortable or feels natural, as this is counterproductive. You are not trying to recreate the ghastly sensation of being winded by a blow to the stomach.

Repeat this for up to ten times; the sound of your breathing should resemble that of an angry bull preparing to charge! If you feel at all dizzy or uncomfortable, then stop and return to normal breathing. Just as a good hearty laugh makes you feel more alive and alert, so too will the bellows breath as it stimulates the brain. The doctors are quite right when they say that laughter is the best medicine.

The cooling breath

This is not dissimilar to the actions of cats and dogs when they stick out their tongues to cool themselves on a hot day, and it is very effective when your body feels overheated, whether through illness, hot weather or central heating.

Sit comfortably and stick out your tongue a little way (though not to the degree that you would for the lion posture; your tongue should not feel stretched). Curl the outer sides of your tongue inwards to form a funnel. Some people cannot 'roll' their tongues in this way, but even a slight inward curve will be effective. Close your eyes and breathe in along this funnel. It should feel lovely and cool. Retain this breath for a few seconds, bringing your tongue in and closing your mouth. Exhale slowly through your nostrils. Think of the process as a cooling system, bringing in cool air and taking hot air out in a continuous cycle. Repeat three times.

The victorious breath (*ujjayi*)

To do this exercise, you must learn to partially close your glottis. This is located at the top of the windpipe between the vocal chords. We naturally close and open our glottis during speech, and most noticeably so when we utter a glottal stop. A glottal stop is a plosive speech sound we make when, for instance, we pronounce the word 'butter' but drop the 'tt' sound. Try it and you will hear a gentle sound emanating from your throat; this is the sound of the glottis closing and opening. In *ujjayi* you seek to make this noise continuous by controlling the breath and keeping it steady.

Begin by standing in the tadasana and lock your chin into the jugular notch. This chin lock is called the *jalandhara* and assists in the process of retaining the breath. Now breath in slowly and deeply, hold for perhaps five seconds, and release in a slow, controlled manner, keeping your glottis partially shut. If the sound wavers, then your exhalation is unsteady. Repeat five times, and, if you concentrate, the sound will become steadier.

This exercise is called the 'victorious breath' because it is said to instill courage. It will certainly remind you of an animal gearing itself up to go on the rampage! It is also good for circulation and clearing the nose and throat, which, in a polluted world, is a victory in itself.

Control over responses

Yoga will not change everything. You will still be you, and feel anger, joy, misery and despair, just like you always did. What yoga can do, however, is give you the power to control your responses to huge events, to rein in powerful emotions and work out what to do with them rather than let them wreak havoc. How many times have you dearly wished that, rather than fly into a rage and shout out what is on your mind, you could wait till you were calm? Or stop and think about the consequences before you get carried along on a wave of excitement? Yoga can give you the power to look before you leap.

Anger/irritation

The traditional ploy for coping with something that causes anger is to close your eyes and count up to ten. In fact, this is not a half bad idea, as it gives you a moment to collect yourself. The yoga way is similar. Stand or sit in a comfortable position, keeping your back straight, and close your eyes. Put your hands together, palms facing, in front of you as if you were about to pray and focus on your breathing, taking deeper and slower breaths each time.

As you descend into a more peaceful state you will feel that the edge has been taken off your anger and that you can examine the cause of it in a more level-headed and positive manner.

Panic/anxiety

Panic usually occurs at a time when you need to act. Unfortunately, panic is the very thing that will prevent you from being able to do so; a state of affairs that will induce even more anxiety! To calm yourself down and get your mental house in order, you need to calm down your heart and breathing. Again, close your eyes and focus on slowing and deepening each breath. If you are sitting at your desk put your hands flat down onto the surface and visualize your panic as an electrical charge that is coursing from your brain, down through your body. Each time you exhale, feel some of that charge exiting through your hands and discharging itself in the work surface. Gradually you will feel calm enough to act.

NB: It is essential that you filter out distractions while you do this exercise, and refrain from mentally 'hurrying' yourself up.

Good/exciting news

Oddly, this can be as stressful as bad news and, once the initial euphoria has worn off, leave you feeling as flat as a pancake and very anticlimactic. To keep yourself in check, put our hands out in front of you, palms downward. Close your eyes and breath slowly. As you exhale, 'push' down with your hands and, as you inhale, allow then to float upwards again.

This exercise will not destroy the pleasure of the experience, merely make your happiness calmer. Thus you will be able to fully take it in, and all its implications.

Ultimately, the yoga aim is to treat great emotion with objectivity. Almost as if you were an impartial observer. Even if you never manage this, these exercises will help you to feel that *you* are in control of them, rather than vice versa.

Yoga hygiene

Cleanliness is next to Godliness, according to the old saying, and it is also next to yoga. The ancient yogis set out very strict instructions about cleansing the body prior to practise. Cleanliness and order are very important to concentration. Consider how difficult it is to work at a desk piled high with papers and assorted rubbish, or to sit down and relax when you really feel that you could do with a bath! Recently there has been a lot of interest in *Feng Shui*, the Oriental art of laying out a home so that it is in harmony with the people who live in it. One of the most fundamental principles of Feng Shui is to avoid unnecessary clutter as this stops up the flow of energy in the home, and to sleep in a room that, ideally, contains only a bed, in order to get proper rest. The yogic knew all this long ago, and devised a series of purification practises to cleanse the body.

The cleansing breath (*kapalabhati*)

To begin, sit in the thunderbolt or half-lotus position and

take a few moments to relax. Breath through your nose and from your diaphragm. When you are ready, take a deep inward breath through your nostrils and then exhale sharply, in a single gust, by contracting your diaphragm. Make sure that you exhale all the air from your lungs. It will sound a bit like a sneeze. Now repeat this process up to ten times, and then relax.

This is a good exercise for clearing the sinuses and boosting the blood circulation.

Another way to do achieve this cleanliness is to stand up straight, with your feet slightly apart. Take a long deep breath and swing your arms above and beyond your head, keeping them straight. Your whole body should be curved backwards to form the shape of a shallow backward C. Now bring your arms round towards your feet in a single movement, and, as you do so, exhale sharply by contracting the diaphragm. Again, make sure that you get all the air out of your lungs in this single exhalation. This is more vigorous exercise than the previous one, so do not attempt to repeat it ten times. About three to five times is more than sufficient.

Perhaps one of the best ways to feel that you have really given your lungs a good clean is to practise breathing exercises beside the sea or a river or stream. These areas are rich in negative ions which help us to feel very refreshed and rejuvenated. Areas where there is a lot of pollution are filled with positive ions which tend to make us feel tired. The last ten years has seen the introduction of ionisers into some workplaces. These machines convert positive ions into negative ones, and the workforce from a sleepy lot to a wide-awake crew. Or at least, so the theory goes, though many people have found them to be enormously beneficial.

Compartmentalisation

Because we lead such busy lives, with so many different demands made of us, many of us feel that our we are living a compartmentalised existence. There is a compartment that is our working life. We change clothes and even personalities, to enter this compartment, becoming harder perhaps, sending out signals of capability and commitment that the inner self may not really feel. Another compartment is home, where we change personalities again, and become more open and loving. This may be the one compartment in which we feel that we are truly being ourselves. There are other compartments, such as the one wherein we meet friends, perhaps more than one group of friends. Little wonder then that we often feel as if our lives are confusing and disconnected, and that there is little room for us to be ourselves.

An interesting way of looking at ourselves is to picture the body as a series of skins, like those of an onion.

Sometimes we peel away these skins to reveal our inner selves, while at other times we put them all back on again. It is a way of reconciling all the different aspects of our lives. Consider the outer layer as the outer physical body, the one that most people see and react to. Within this is the inner physical layer, the layer where all the breathing and digestion goes on. Within that is the conscious mind, where our day to day thinking goes on, where the words that spring out of our physical mouths are generated. Within this is the subconscious, the place where we hoard our memories and work out our feelings, and where our sense of free will comes from. And deep, deep inside this is our inner self, the very core of our being, which is the only part of us that can truly connect with the universe.

Thinking of the body in this way can be a wonderful tool for meditation, and is also a rather soothing thought when you feel as if you are somehow disconnected from yourself. Next time you find yourself in the midst of a busy office, feeling stressed and as if you are putting on an act and wondering how you can be the same person who climbed a mountain at the weekend, or read your children a long, exciting story last night, and did all the actions and felt wonderfully happy, remember that you have simply donned a few more layers this morning and are still the same person inside.

Chapter Seven

The Chakras

According to yogic philosophy, the spine marks a central channel, the sushumna, which runs through the body. Situated along this channel are seven energy centres or chakras. The word chakra is a Hindu word meaning 'nerve centre' or 'wheel'. Each chakra has an individual 'character' and corresponds to a certain colour, element, mood and activity, as well as having a unique function in promoting bodily health. The positions of the chakras correspond to plexuses in the body, and to the acupuncture charts of traditional Chinese medicine. It is possible that there was the equivalent of chakras in ancient Western philosophy as the nature of each seems well suited. For example, the anahata chakra, which governs emotions, is situated near the heart; the internal organ to which we ascribe so much emotional feeling, describing ourselves as having a heavy heart, a fluttering heart, even a heart that is on fire!

The chakras are located where the *namis*, the carriers of

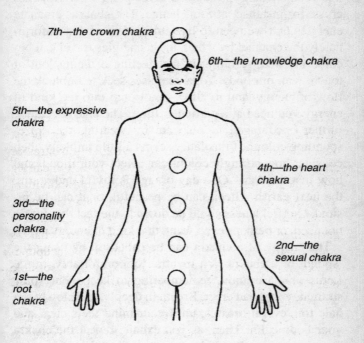

7th—the crown chakra

6th—the knowledge chakra

5th—the expressive chakra

4th—the heart chakra

3rd—the personality chakra

2nd—the sexual chakra

1st—the root chakra

The seven major chakras

Prana, the life force, cross. This is not unlike the belief that cosmic energy is sourced at the point where leylines cross, for instance, at Stonehenge. The chakras emanate energies that we need to live fulfilled lives, but unfortunately the channel by which these energies travel can become blocked, resulting in that feeling of being 'out of touch' with our body. Yoga exercises seek to unblock the flow of energy, and to allow you to tap into the kind of energy you need at a particular time. The chakras can be further encouraged to resonate by wearing the corresponding colour. If this latter seems a little unlikely, then consider how strongly colour can affect your mood, and how that can vary. One day orange is joyful and warm, the next garish. Green can be peaceful, or it can be insipid. Our fickleness could be down to the fact that we do not need, or perhaps even want, that kind of energy today.

The energy of a chakra can be called up by using the 'sound' of a chakra as a mantra. Sit comfortably, in the Lotus or a variation, remembering to keep your spine straight, your head erect. Breath in deeply, and slowly exhale for several breaths, until your mind feels clear and your body calm. Then, as you exhale, repeat the chakra sound, then slowly inhale. Repeat several times, concentrating on the location of the chakra, until its energy can be felt. You can concentrate on a specific chakra, or move from the base of the spine to the crown of the head, chanting each mantra in turn. Some people describe the effect of this as being akin to a series of lights coming on, culminating in a dazzling glow at the top. Others describe is as a series of bells, getting gradually higher and purer in note. In time, you will learn to sound the notes internally. If you prefer to see than hear, you can do the same exercise but visualise the colours rather than sound the notes.

Stop if you begin to feel dizzy or disoriented, return to a normal breathing pattern and return to the mantra another time. Initially chanting still and soothes as it aids the sourcing of energy; with practice it can become the key to the meditative state.

Maladhara

Found at the base of the spine, the perineum plexus, this chakra is close to the groin area. Despite this, it is not the chakra that promotes sexual energy, but rather strengthens attributes such as security and stability, and sharpens instinct. It is related to the element of earth. 'Mula' means root, and 'adhara' means support, so this is the chakra that gives us that grounded, content within ourselves feeling. If you find that you constantly seek reassurances from people, or rely on props like money, possessions or status to make you feel secure, this is the chakra you should be tapping into. It is also the chakra that will sharpen up your sense of smell. The colour red will stimulate this chakra, or chant the sound 'LAM' to call up its energy.

Swadisthana

In Sanskrit, Swadisthana means 'place of origin', and is located in the mid-abdomen at the prostatic plexus. This is the chakra that promotes sexual and sociable energy, making its colour, orange, ideal party wear. However, this energy can have negative connotations, such as jealousy or an overemphasis on the sexual side of relationships. Homing in on this chakra, either by visualisation or chanting its mantra, VAM, can help to keep this energy positive, and push tilted sexual emotions back into an upright position.

This chakra's element is water, and is the source of much creative energy. It is also related to the sense of taste.

Manipura

Located in the solar plexus, the *manipuru*, which means 'bright jewel of inner power', is the source of the 'fire in the belly' that propels us to great things. It is related to the element of fire and, according to ancient Chinese wisdom, is the centre of psychic power and the source of 'chi', which means 'life force'. By tapping into this chakra we are stoking the fire of our deepest power. Even conventional medicine cannot fault the logic of the Manipuru; deep breathing, drawing oxygen into the region of the solar plexus, nourishes the organs of the abdomen, which are essential to good health. Take a deep, deep breath and feel your lower body respond.

The colour for this chakra is yellow, and its effect is akin to that of an antidepressant, without the side-effects. It boosts your inner confidence, but not by means of the ego, which is flattered by external agents only. If bright primary yellow is not your colour, try a darker, golden or ochre hue as these work just as well. Despite being such a happy colour, who doesn't respond to the yellow of buttercups or feel cheered by the glow of lamplight?, it is a colour we rarely wear. Could this be at the root of our famous Western lack of self-esteem?

The sound for this chakra is RAM, an appropriately thunderous note for such a superpower chakra.

Anahata

This is the chakra that brings harmony to your emotions and the breath of life, which is very apt as it is located near the heart on the pulmonary plexus. Focusing on this centre can promote a sense of love for all living things, which will not only make you feel good, it will give your health a boost too. Think of the way that love can put a spring in your step, compared to the brooding, weighty feeling generated by hatred.

Green, also acknowledged by practitioners of colour therapy and Feng Shui as inducive to peace, is the colour for anahata harmony. It provides serenity and is perfect for a frenzied day of Christmas shopping or a highly-charged day at the office. However, it is quite an emotional colour and is not advisable for situations where you may want to keep your feelings in check. Perhaps this is the reason green is considered unlucky at Christian weddings, lest it cause too many outbreaks of tears?

Anahata, which means 'self-sustaining' is related to the element air. Meditation upon this chakra involves focusing on the air that sustains life an that life sustains. Oxygen keeps us alive, we convert it into carbon dioxide, which keeps plants alive, who covert it back into oxygen; air is a never-ending cycle of life. The mantra for this chakra is YAM.

Vissudha

Located at the branchial or pharyngeal plexus, this chakra is near the throat. It promotes steadiness and balance and is essential for keeping a level head. It is also the chakra of concentration and logic and its energy will induce fruitful study, whether you be about to embark on a diet of exams or wish to coolly weigh up the pros and cons of a new relationship or a new direction in life.

Wear blue to tap into Vissudha's energy, which will also help you to rid your mind of resentments and bones of contention, the very things which can block clear thought. It is also great for bending your mind round complex concepts. Its sound is HAM.

Anja

Naturally the head is related to the mind, but also to the spirit. Here the energies are not directed solely at earth-bound needs and problems, but those of achieving one-ness and spiritual reality.

The anja is the 'third eye', set between your eyes at the choroid plexus, which has control of all thoughts, whether incoming or outgoing. Its element is the mind, and it is considered, in yogic philosophy, to be the vertical eye of wisdom, as opposed to conventional, horizontal wisdom, and as such is related to the Divine. Our deepest insights, not just into the apparent world but that which is beyond it, derive from here. Wear or visualise indigo to stimulate your intuition and intellect, or chant the mantra OM (pronounced ah-oh-mm) in a shorter, lower tone than you will use for the next chakra.

The anja is connected to the hypothalamus and pituitary glands, and its energy can be channelled towards regulating mind and body reactions, and ensuring that the messages your brain receives are not misleading.

Sahasraha

This means 'a thousand petals' and is visualised as a thousand petalled lotus emanating from the crown of the head. In yogic texts it is symbolised as a thousand rays of light that create an effect similar to the halo of Christian symbolism. Located at the highest point of the body, it is fitting that sahasraha relates to the purest, most spiritual instincts of man. Its colour is white, the colour of angels and light, and meditation upon this centre produces that highly prized feeling of oneness with the universe. It is the link between the individual and the universal self and its mantra is the longer, higher sounding of OM.

Warning!:

The colours detailed above should not be seen as 'lucky' colours, or adhered to religiously according to mood: an orange dress will not transform you into a flirt! Avoid getting trapped in neurotic superstitions, such as blue for exams, as this will only make you unhappy. You will seek these colours naturally, in all probability you already do to some extent. It can help to visualise colours rather than wear them if you are inclined towards superstition. During a hectic day, visualise a field of green, or if you cannot get your mind straight about all those facts and figures, close your eyes and think of a boat, painted the colour of a summer sky.

Kundalini

'Kundalini' means 'the coiled serpent' which is said to sleep at the base of the spine, where the Muladhara chakra is located. Intense meditation can be used to awaken this serpent, which is sometimes described as being like a power cable, causing it to rise up through the chakras and is said to release great psychic powers when it reaches the thousand-petalled lotus of the sahasraha chakra. Intriguingly enough, this practise is warned against as being too dangerous for the uninitiated. The yogics of old advise you strongly to seek the guidance of a someone highly trained in the art of kundalini rather than attempt it alone.

Chapter Eight

Meditation

Regular practise of the asanas and breathing exercises
will induce a more positive frame of mind, not just during
the exercises but throughout daily life. You will find that
you are less prone to mood swings, and that you feel less
at the mercy of external forces as you have developed an
increased degree of inner strength. To an extent you have
developed self-mastery. This may be as far as you wish to
go. In time, however, you may wish to take this process of
self-mastery a stage further through the practise of Raja
yoga, the king of all yogas. Raja yoga helps to still the
vrittis, which are the thought waves, allowing you to
know your true self.

Knowing yourself the yoga way is quite a different
thing from knowing your habits, likes and dislikes. In
fact, having fixed ideas about yourself can often obscure
your true nature, as you shut yourself off from experiences, or tell yourself, in advance, how you are going to
react. For instance, if you believe that you are an impa-

tient person who needs fast results, then you will become frustrated by the slow results of yoga, and perhaps give up without giving yourself a chance. If, instead, you try turning this assumption about yourself on its head, and tell yourself that actually you have infinite reserves of patience, you will surprise yourself by having just such reserves. Bear this in mind when you practise your asanas too. If you believe that you are stiff and unsupple, the exercises will be tough. If, instead, you convince yourself that there is a super-supple person inside you just itching to get out, you will begin to feel a real difference. It is important to approach yoga with an open mind, and to shed feelings of pride and desire. This is called 'transcending the ego'. Far from being the self-abnegation that it sounds, transcending your ego is actually extremely liberating.

If you are still resistant to the idea of finding your true self, perhaps because you feel that you are already very well acquainted, thank you very much, then consider how many times in your life you have felt that you are acting 'out of character'. An occasion perhaps when you drank more alcohol than usual, said things you didn't mean, or had unaccountable mood swings. We do this when we are unhappy and out of touch with ourselves, usually due to stress and being constantly bombarded by external pressures that give us no time or freedom to look into ourselves. Certainly there are few people who can claim that they never behave differently with different people and in different environments, sometimes endorsing opinions that they do not believe in, and acting against their instincts. Occasions like this often leave us feeling unworthy, and lacking in integrity. The impulse to behave this way generally arises from a lack of self-confidence and a lack of a sense of our own selves.

Now consider how it feels to be happily in love. This is not to be confused with the intense infatuation characterised by highs and lows, but the later, more relaxed stage. When in love, we feel as if we have found our destiny and that everything in the world is in its right place. We feel slightly removed from ordinary life, and less thrown by external events. We feel that we can cope with everything, from big red electricity bills to three weeks of flu. In fact, being in love makes us more immune to disease, and makes our skin clearer and our eyes sparkling. Yet, for all that we are removed, we feel as if our senses have been fine tuned, making us alert to sounds and colours, so that we feel we are really seeing the world around us. We feel alive and at the centre of our being. Discovering your true self produces similar feelings of awareness and oneness.

Some people feel afraid of uncovering their true selves, regarding it as a sort of frightening therapy process wherein they will be forced to confront aspects of their nature with which they are uncomfortable. This is not so.

Raja yoga is not a form of therapy in the psychoanalytic sense. Rather it is tapping into the essence of your being, the spirit from which you sprang. Indeed, this realization of the inner self can provide enormous support when dealing with difficult personal problems, and a way of giving yourself temporary release from them.

Even if we are free of deep troubles and have sufficient confidence to be ourselves, we all live in a very manic, busy world, which bombards us with multifarious messages about how we should live and what we should think. Women especially tend to feel that they are pulled this way and that by contradictory demands, to be feminine but independent, good mothers but also good workers, and so on. Sometimes we need a touchstone, a talisman for instance, a place, or even a person, towards which we can reach when we feel the need to 'touch base' and work things out. In ancient communities there would be wise woman or man who could counsel those who felt out of sorts and confused. Our equivalent today, perhaps, is the agony aunt! When we achieve self-knowledge we become our own touchstone, the person we can rely on.

Think of the mind as a lake and the vrittis as ripples. Every stray thought causes a ripple, making it harder to see down through the water at your real self. The objective is to still the mind till it is like the surface of a smooth, mirror-like lake. Meditation is the yoga way of achieving this inner stillness. There are three stages,

Pratyahara, Dharana and Dhyana, to be completed before the self-realization can be achieved, though it is entirely up to the individual how far along this path they wish to go, and at what speed.

Withdrawal of senses (*pratyahara*)

The fifth limb of yoga is pratyahara, which means 'gathering inwards'. It involves the withdrawal of senses, or, to put it in more straightforward terms, releasing the mind from its domination by the senses. This does not mean numbing the senses so that our taste, sight, hearing, sense of touch and smell are so impaired that we cannot enjoy the outside world! Rather it means controlling our reactions to sense impressions. The value of this can be seen immediately if you consider the sense impressions we receive from a headache; being able to distance ourselves from that misery would be a wonderful thing indeed. However, it also has value in connection with everyday sense impressions as it enables us to fully tune into our mind and analyse its workings.

In fact, we control our senses on a regular basis without actually realising it. Sprinters, for example, sometimes talk about the 'white tunnel' they seem to run through when their mind's energy is totally locked into winning the race. The sounds of the crowd, even the presence of the other runners, is screened out so that they can concentrate. On a more mundane level, think of reading an enthralling novel and suddenly looking up to find that the daylight has faded, the fire has gone out, and you have been feeling cold without even noticing.

Our sense organs are not infallible, and can easily be 'tricked'. A hypnotist, for example, can convince a person to eat an onion and enjoy it as if were a lovely juicy apple. While this is done in the cause of entertainment, hypnosis can be used to achieve positive ends, such as giving up smoking. In this case, the hypnotist persuades the patient's senses to loathe the smell and taste of the habit they previously felt that they enjoyed, and plants in the mind the belief that smoking is no longer needed as an emotional prop. However, the effects of such hypnosis do not always last and the reason for this is that the anti-smoking impetus has been planted in the mind by someone else. An idea created from within is much stronger, because you are the one in control, and the one who can reinforce it.

Faith healing works in much the same way, and is more powerful because it prompts the person being 'healed' to take control. The healer has no 'magic touch', but by convincing them that he has, their mind believes the body to be healed and responds to sense impressions differently and becomes less overwhelmed by them. The result is often a 'miraculous' reduction in pain and discomfort.

Controlling our senses the yoga way requires no such external intervention, but it does require a lot of practice.

The *Bhagavad Gita* recommends an almost scientific approach of practising the observation of your sense impressions almost as if they did not belong to you. The Scottish poet Iain Crichton Smith, when he suffered a long illness, feared that he would never again hear the 'inner handle' of his mind. The 'inner handle' to which he referred was that part of himself, deep inside, that could distance itself from the his senses and emotions in order to observe them and capture their essence in poetry. His illness barred his way by dominating him with miserable and insistent sense impressions.

An exercise that can help you to tap into this inner self is to sit very quietly and sink into the experience of simply sitting. Close your eyes and be alert to every sound and smell, the distant roar of traffic, the hum of a lawnmower, the scent of the air coming through the window. Now think of yourself hearing and smelling these things, think of how the sounds are not a part of you but threads of information that your ear transmits to your brain. Think of the inner you that receives these threads of information, and rather than interpret the messages, deciding whether you like them or not, or letting your mind drift off on thoughts and memories triggered by them, just home in on that inner self.

On a practical note, try this exercise the next time you have a headache. Think of the pain and what part of your head is sending this message to your brain. Again, think of it as a thread of information, like a radio wave, that your inner self is receiving. Home in on that inner self and you will find that the pain recedes from the front of your consciousness.

With practise you will eventually be able to tap into the gaps between thoughts, moments of utter tranquillity to which we very rarely get access. This is *pratyahara*, the first stage of turning inwards and the first step towards self-realization, which is called *samedhi*.

Concentration (*dharana*) and contemplation (*dhyana*)

The sixth limb of yoga is concentration; the art of focusing on a single idea or object. This sounds simple enough, but in fact we rarely achieve it. Consider how often you forget what you were about to say, or lose track of a train of thought. This happens because the mind tends to flit from one thought to the other, especially when we become adults and have so much more to think about. Children, by comparison, are often to be seen utterly absorbed in a project, say a painting or even simply staring out the window at the shapes of clouds. Adults tend to be wary about throwing themselves into a task in case there is something more important that they should be thinking about. Women are especially prone to this, particularly if they have young children, as they develop almost an extra sense that is forever on the alert for signals of their offspring's distress. The drawback of all this mental activity is that it can be irritating being unable to concentrate, and therefore stressful, and can also hamper our chances of success in life.

We refer to successful people as 'single-minded' and 'focused', meaning that they know what they want and concentrate on getting it. This sometimes carries with it the negative connotation of meaning that the person is overambitious, even ruthless, and has little time or thought for anything other than their personal success. Single-minded people, according to popular perception, stay in the office till all hours, take work home, and ignore their families. But in fact, being focused need not be negative at all. Sportspeople, performers and artists all need to be able to focus in order to achieve. A distracted artist would never complete any paintings, a distracted athlete fail to win a single race. Concentration is the key to mental and physical success.

It is also the key to revelation. Mystics have claimed to see great and wonderful visions through intense prayer or meditation. St Theresa of Avila, the founder of the Carmelite order, found that constant devotion through prayer enabled her to feel at one with her creator. To this day, the Carmelites devote much of their waking life to prayer, often with a purpose, such as praying for the victims of war, in the belief that their meditations will generate a spiritual energy that will help to alleviate human misery. On a secular level, it is believed that the great thinkers and inventors of past ages came upon their discoveries through meditation upon a single object or idea, projecting the power of the whole mind in one direction. It is often said that the hardest part of invention is working out what to invent; the hows and whys are quite straightforward by comparison. Consider how James Watt came to discover the power of steam. From gazing at the steam coming out of a kettle, he came to realize that here was a source of energy that could be exploited for the benefit of mankind. Had he been staring at it but thinking about what to have for dinner, or what the weather was likely to be like tomorrow, the great age of steam may have been severely delayed.

Concentration can also lead to personal fulfilment, if only because it makes us more productive and thereby allows us more time away from the workplace. It also enables us to pay attention to, and prioritise, the different segments of our lives. Many people with busy careers find that they waste their leisure time worrying about work, resulting in a failure to give family and personal affairs their due attention. Dharana helps us to plug our thoughts back into every area of our lives. This is called *samprajanya*, which means awareness of all things.

Practising dharana and dhyana
To practice dharana, ensure first of all that you are sitting comfortably, in the thunderbolt or half-lotus for instance.

The half lotus

If you are uncomfortable your mind will constantly be distracted by negative signals, and the exercise will become pointless. Tale a few minutes to relax, breathing deeply from your diaphragm. Concentrating on your breathing will assist in the process of clearing your mind. Now find a small object to concentrate upon. A giant hillside or full-size painting will have your eyes, and mind, darting all over the place! Select something like a pretty stone, a flower, or a small photograph, something which you like and will make you feel positive. You might want to keep certain objects aside specifically for this purpose, perhaps a piece of sea-softened glass that you found on a beautiful beach or a small sculpture made by a child. The object does not need to have religious or talismanic significance; it is simply a tool for aiding concentration.

A good beginner's exercise is to take the object of your choice, let us say it is a seashell, and imagine how you would paint it. Examine the colours, the way that certain hues repeat themselves in patterns, and how the texture varies from smooth to rough. Now close your eyes and run your fingers round and inside the shell, feeling the textures. Bring it close to your nose and inhale the scent. Think of where it came from, how it was washed ashore by the sea and how the waves softened it over time. Think of the creature that once inhabited it. As you do this exercise you will come to appreciate the essence of the shell itself, and be able to summon it up almost as a single thought. The shell will become a fusion of its colours, textures, smell and history. Learning to focus on the essence of an object or idea is called Dhyana, which means contemplation.

A good way to build up your concentration skills throughout the day is to try a little Zen living. Pour yourself a glass of water. Allow the tap to run till the water is very cold, and listen to the sound of the water as it fills the glass, and feel its coldness seeping through to your hand. As you drink, think about the feel of it in your mouth, the sensation of refreshing coolness as you swallow. Think of how this pure substance is acting to purify your system, helping your kidneys to flush out toxins and helping to keep your body hydrated. By the time you have finished, your mind will feel as refreshed as your body.

Eventually you will learn to spot focus on an object. To do this, locate the central spot of the object and focus your gaze there rather than allow it to wander around. Imagine your sight as two lines that converge at this spot and keep that point of convergence steady. Allow your facial muscles and shoulders to relax; screwing up your eyes will only make you tense. Try not to be frustrated by the fact that, inevitably, your first attempts will be hindered by your thoughts' tendency to waver off course. Do not be discouraged, or even the least bit surprised, if your mind starts working out next month's disposable income or making a mental 'things to do' list for the weekend. Simply acknowledge the fact that you have wandered and steer your mind back. Don't stop to analyse these thoughts and where they came from, simply push them away. Some people find that a physical gesture, such as batting the thoughts away like flies, can help.

You will gradually become better and better at batting away stray thoughts, and your mental straying will begin to diminish. Initially it requires effort, but it will become effortless.

Visualization

Practising dharana with your eyes shut helps to control the senses and can thus make focusing easier. Most of us are naturally very good at visualization and can close our eyes and summon up images in our mind's eye at will. We do it when we daydream and when we dream in our sleep. Honing your visualization skills will not only benefit your ability to meditate, it will also enhance your life, enabling you to store up 'snapshots' that make you happy or inspire you, to be recalled whenever you want them.

The candle meditation

This exercise will help to develop your visualization skills. The selection of a lit candle as meditative object is a popular one because in many people's minds it is synonymous with positive ideas such as hope, faith and peace. Place your lit candle about a foot in front of you on the floor. Gaze into the flame and study the way that it flickers. Look at the shape and colour of the candle itself and take note of how the wax begins to melt and whether it drips. Once you feel that your thoughts are totally absorbed by the candle, and that its image fills your mind, close your eyes. Continue to 'see' the candle, not as a frozen image, but as it flickers in front of you. As soon as the image starts to fade or become distorted, open your eyes to refresh your visual memory, and then shut them again. With patient practise you will no longer need the candle.

Your mind will be able to summon up its essence unaided.

When you are doing a visualization exercise, try to focus on the space between your eyebrows. This is the location of the anja chakra, the third eye, which is the centre of intellectual and intuitive activity. Learning to focus here will stimulate this energy centre, and help you to reach the mindstate beyond everyday thought, the gaps between thoughts, which is the state of self-realization.

A visualization journey

This requires you to lie on your back in the corpse posture. Make sure that you are not too cold or warm and that your body feels comfortable as this will take some time. Take a series of deep breaths and let yourself be heavy into the floor. As you exhale, let all your thoughts go with the outward breath. Close your eyes and look through your third eye. Think of yourself standing on a beach. The sea is in front of you and you are looking out towards the horizon. It is an early summer's morning and the sky is very clear and blue. You can feel the warmth of the sun on your face and the soft white sand under your bare feet. Listen to the sound of the waves gently breaking and hear the cry of gulls circling over the water. You are alone and feel very peaceful. Step closer to the water, to where the sand is damp, and you will become aware of the slight undertow of the tide tugging at the sand under your feet. Stand here for a minute, and breathe in the odour of the sea.

Now turn to your right and you will see the shore curving round to form a bay. The water there is very shallow and you can see the ribs of sand underneath the gently undulating water. Walk towards the bay and step into the water till it reaches your shins. Feel the icy coolness of it against your skin and the way that the sand shifts under your feet, clouding the waters where you walk. Step back onto dry land and feel the sand sticking to your shins and feet, and how the warmth of the sun dries your skin. Turn so that you are facing away from the sea towards sand dunes. Now climb one. It is steep and your feet plunges into the soft warm sand. Grab hold of grasses to pull yourself up and feel how your muscles work to pull you upwards.

When you reach the top you are a little out of breath, so stop and look at the landscape in front of you. Green fields stretch as far as you can see, rising to gentle hills in the distance. To your right you see a group of ancient, summer lush trees. The grass is soft underfoot and as you look you spot wild flowers growing in clusters. You see red poppies and white meadowsweet. You feel a breeze blow across the side of your face, and you notice how the grass blades bend gently under it in waves. You hear the rustle of leaves in the trees. In the distance a bird swoops over the fields and flies towards the horizon, dwindling to a tiny speck. Inhale the fragrance of the grass and trees, the smell of the earth warming up under the sun.

Now turn to your right and walk towards the trees. Feel the coolness of their shadows as you walk through them and the way the sunlight glances onto your skin through gaps in the branches. From above comes the soft twitter of birds. Sit down at the base of a tree trunk and lean your back against it. Feel the roughness of the bark against your skin and the grass beneath you. Close your eyes and listen to the sounds around you. Relax and just be there for a few minutes. When you are ready, allow your mind to accustom itself to where you really are. Feel the floor under your body, think of where the walls and ceiling are in relation to you, and gradually open your eyes.

You may want to make changes to this journey, perhaps adapting it to fit a landscape that is known to you, or create one of your own. Perhaps you would prefer mountains in the distance, or to begin beside a gushing stream. The important thing is to relax and not worry about details. You don't need to be able to see every blade of grass and whorl of tree bark, just feel the essence of the place and create a sense of spatial awareness as to where things are in relation to you. It might help to record your journey on a cassette and let your voice guide you along.

Visualization and the body

Visualization can be used to stimulate the body as well as withdrawing inside it. Modern medicine is increasingly coming to accept that there is a great deal of truth in the old phrase 'mind over matter'. Intense mental concentration on a body part can actually stimulate a physical response as we know from the work of hypnotists and faith healers, who 'tell' the mind how to respond to a sense impression. However, if you are able to 'tell' your mind how to respond without external assistance, the effect is much increased. A simple demonstration of this fact is to do the lemon test. Close your eyes and think of a ripe yellow lemon. Think of its waxy surface, feel it in your hands. Now take a sharp knife and cut into the fruit. Smell the sharp tang of the lemon juice as you cut yourself a small slice. Now bring it to your mouth, and the scent becoming stronger. Bite into the fruit and feel the juice on your tongue. Now take careful note of what your mouth is actually doing. Yes, it is salivating in response to the idea of that sharp, citrus taste.

Now try concentrating on your scalp, a part of the body that we rarely touch. As you focus intently on that area you will being to feel your nerve-endings tingle. This ability to home in on a part of your body is used in meditation upon the chakras, and can produce amazing results.

Nidra

Nidra' is the name of a meditation exercise wherein you focus on every part of your body in turn to induce a deep state of relaxation, similar to the sensation you feel just before you fall asleep. It is a wonderful exercise to practise at the end of, or even in the middle of, a hectic day, as it will make you feel very refreshed, as if you have had a night's sleep. Begin by lying on your back, in the corpse posture. Make sure that you are comfortable and that you are neither too hot nor too cold. Close your eyes and breath steadily, listening to your breath. You don't need to take deep breaths. Just relax. It can help to imagine that you have entered a zone of non-time. Tell yourself that it will be exactly the same time when you come out of this exercise as you when you began it. Of course it is untrue, but the thought is a very seductive one when you feel that you have been at the mercy of the ticking clock all day.

When you are ready, begin with your scalp. Focus on it till it begins to tingle, and then slowly move your focus down to your forehead. Don't flex and relax as you did for the corpse posture, just concentrate on each area in turn. You will be amazed at how your body reacts, almost as if a warm ray was being shone across it. Keep breathing naturally and gently, and move down your face. Don't think about what each part of your body means to you, or how it looks, just feel it, as if you were occupying the space just inside it. Move down to your shoulders and then focus on each upper arm, each elbow and hand in turn. Move back up to your chest, down your torso to your abdomen, and then down to each thigh, knee and foot in turn. Try to keep your thoughts from wandering off, as this will make you sleepy. The act of concentrating on each part in turn will keep you alert, and you will experience the delicious sensation of being entirely relaxed but awake to enjoy it.

When you are finished, give yourself a moment or two to 'come to', and don't attempt something too urgent or active immediately afterwards. Give yourself time to re-accustom itself to the world.

The art of noise

Sounds have a profound effect upon us. They can stimulate deep emotions and even prompt physical responses. Some sounds prompt memories, the strain of a long-forgotten hymn can transport someone back to their schooldays, while the rattle of familiar keys in the lock can make a person feel reassured and happy. However, it is not all to do with memory. Beautiful music can move us to tears or uplift us so that we feel our heart 'soar' with the melody. The sound of waves breaking on a shore induces a sense of peace, while the rumble of thunder makes us alert, perhaps even very nervous. And our recall of sounds is generally much better than we realize. We can learn to recognize someone by the sound of their footsteps, and know instinctively when a sound is 'out of place', such as an unfamiliar creak on a floorboard or a false note in someone's voice.

Concentrating using sound is a viable alternative for anyone who finds visualization difficult. In some cases, this latter is simply a case of being unable to concentrate fully and will improve with practise. For others, however, it will remain difficult, because the person has a better developed aural memory than a visual one. A way of determining this is to imagine a tennis ball. Picture it, concentrating on its rough texture, its colour and its shape. Keep concentrating until that picture is fully in your mind. Now imagine you have thrown the tennis ball against a wall and it has bounced off and along the pavement. Can you hear it? If you find the listening substantially easier, and more absorbing, than the looking, you may want to try dharana exercises using sound rather than images.

Hamsa

Hamsa is a Sanskrit word meaning bird, and the hamsa meditation involves visualizing a bird in flight. Take a few deep breaths and fill your mind with the image of a clear blue sky. Now picture a bird soaring across it, watch it swoop and soar across your field of vision. Take a deep breath and as you inhale say the word 'ham', and as you exhale, say 'sa'. Repeat this several times and just allow the bird to fly away, but keep visualizing that sky. Keep up this gentle chanting for several minutes, and you will find that your mind has cleared itself of intruding thoughts and is absorbed by the blue and the notes of the chant.

Inner Sounds (Nadas)

Concentrating on inner sounds is another way of shutting out external sounds and thoughts. It also develops increased awareness of your own body and its internal workings. Begin by placing your fingers over your ears; this will shut out external noise. Close your eyes and allow your breathing to relax. As your mind becomes still you will become aware of a steady surging, rumbling sound. In fact, you will be amazed by the noise in there! Keep listening carefully, remembering to keep your body relaxed and your mind focused. Beneath this rumbling sound you will eventually discern subtler sounds. As they become apparent, hone your focus in towards them. If your mind begins to wander, switch back to the louder sounds, then back to the subtler ones behind them. Ultimately your mind will become absorbed by these quieter sounds and you will experience a deep sense of serenity. When you come out of this exercise you may feel surprised at how quiet the outside world is by comparison.

Don't be discouraged if, the first few times you try this, you hear only the surging sounds. Like all yoga techniques, it requires practise and patience.

Psychic powers

Many yogis claim that yogic meditation can unleash latent psychic powers called Siddhis. However, they warn against the practitioner viewing these powers as an end in themselves as they can lead to pride, which can act as a barrier to the ego-transcendence necessary to achieve Samadhi. Certainly regular yoga meditation will help the mind to think more clearly and this will lead to your becoming more perceptive. Whether this will ever lead to your being able to correctly predict the week's lottery numbers is another matter.

One of the powers that yogics claim is that of extrasensory perception (ESP), where a person is able to sense what is about to happen, for instance, when danger is ahead. Modern research has given more credence to the notion of ESP, and researchers in this area have discovered that the deeply meditative state achieved through Pratyahara produces the slow Alpha waves that are recognised as being conducive to profound and inspirational thought.

In our normal, waking state our brain activity is characterised by Beta waves. When we are deeply asleep, our brain activity settles to slower, fainter waves called Delta waves. However, between waking and sleeping, our brain activity is characterised by waves that are slower than Beta waves but much, much stronger. These are called Alpha waves. This accounts for those unexpected moments of intense lucidity that we can have before we fall asleep, though we are rarely able to take advantage of them as our brain is already dipping into Delta wave activity. The Alpha state can, however, be achieved with conscious effort and people have found that it gives them access to tremendous insights and ideas. Modern mind-management gurus often include a guide as to how to achieve this mindstate in their programmes for personal success. And their methods are not unlike those formulated by the yogis all those millennia ago.

Self-realization (*samadhi*)

Once you master the art of focusing on the essence of a thing, you are ready for the final stage of raja yoga, *samadhi*. This is also known as superconsciousness, and is the state wherein the person meditating feels a oneness with the object of contemplation, and thus with the universe itself. Awareness of the self is transcended. This is not to say that you become numb and lacking in awareness. In fact, the opposite is true. A tremendous sense of peace and wholeness ensues from this state of 'pure existence'. You are unhampered by conscious thoughts and the intrusion of sense impressions, but intensely aware of, and merged with, your surroundings. People who have achieved samadhi describe it as akin to being filled with dazzling white light. An image not unlike depictions of visionary saints being by white rays of heavenly light, representing the Holy Spirit entering the human body.

This super-conscious state should not be dismissed as something that only the very religious can achieve. Nor as something from which only such people will benefit.

Everyone has a spiritual side to their nature, whether they choose to frame it in religious terms or not, and this heightened state need not interfere with any code of belief, whether it be Hinduism or humanism.

Samadhi could be described as being similar to one of those rare and wonderful moments when we truly 'forget ourselves'. Music and art are often cited as the cause of such transcendent experiences and almost everyone can cite one symphony, song or painting that has, at some time, stopped them in their tracks and lifted them to a state 'beyond words'. Religious music and art especially has this ability to uplift people, perhaps because the creators of it are intensely religious themselves and view their work as a form of worship. Giotto, the thirteenth century Italian painter, regarded his works as a way of praising God and to this day his famous Assisi frescoes, with their serene, simplistic quality, are capable of imbuing a sense of peace and spiritual hope in those who gaze upon them. John Taverner, the composer whose work was included in the funeral service of Diana, Princess of Wales, is a devout Christian and his work is characterised by a soaring, other-worldly quality that many find truly inspiring.

Like this moments of elation, the state of samadhi does not last. When we come out of it, it is gone, though it can be returned to, and with increasing ease if you continue with dedication. However, samadhi does not leave you empty-handed. It leaves you with the knowledge that such a super-conscious, blissful state is possible, and the realisation that we are not trapped within ourselves and the confines of our daily consciousness.

Chapter Nine

Yoga and Diet

In the latter half of the 20th century, the pressure to be slim is enormous, and this despite the fact that over two thirds of the planet's population is struggling to find enough to eat. Indeed, western society could almost be described as a fat-intolerant one. Not only do our ideals of beauty, almost without exception, centre on slenderness, but recent research has shown that employers consider being overweight a negative attribute in a prospective employee, and one that disinclines them to offer a job, no matter what the profession. The reason for this is that being overweight is often considered an indication of a person's laziness and lack of self-control.

The sad fact is that many people actually become fat as an indirect result of all this pressure to be thin. Low-calorie, low-fat, high-fibre and other diets have been proved, time and time again, to be unsuccessful in the long term. This is because, when we deprive the body of the fuel it needs, it reacts by lowering the metabolism, believing itself to be in danger of starvation. This reduced metabolism lingers long after the diet is completed, and so, when the dieter returns to former eating patterns, they regain the weight they lost. In fact, many find that they become even heavier than before, and therefore embark on another diet, which reduces their metabolism even further.

Teenagers who enter this vicious cycle of weight loss and gain may reach adulthood never having established regular, healthy eating patterns. Not only can this result in perhaps a lifetime of yo-yo-ing weight, it can also foster a very unhappy relationship with food, to the point that every occasion involving eating becomes a trial, and food become an 'enemy' to be battled with. This may sound extreme, but think of the number of times a day you hear people say that they 'can't eat that' or they 'shouldn't', or finish up a wonderful meal by vowing their determination never to repeat the experience. It has even entered popular culture, with cartoon characters like Snoopy and Garfield announcing from tea-towels and aprons that their 'diet starts on Monday'. We may laugh, but for thousands upon thousands of people, Monday morning really has become a weekly ritual of good intentions, followed by the inevitable failure round about Tuesday lunchtime.

The simple answer is to stop dieting, take more exercise and establish a healthy eating pattern. However, this is a lot easier said than done. Many people fear that if they stopped dieting they would be unable to stop eating and become enormous. Some have little idea of what normal eating patterns are. Plus, the fact that almost every food-stuff is now available in a low-calorie, low-fat format fools people into thinking they can eat twice as much of it. It is a sobering thought that in the United States, where most of these 'diet-friendly' foods are pioneered, over half the population is seriously overweight.

There are other issues too. Many of us, as children, viewed certain kinds of food, such as sweets, as reward foods. Therefore, when we become adults, we treat ourselves with sweets and cakes, or turn to these kinds of foods as a way of comforting ourselves. Thus, if we are depressed by the fact that we have put on weight, we might decide to cheer ourselves up with a tasty, high-calorie snack. Binge-eating, where the person gorges themselves on food, has nothing to do with being greedy. In fact, people who have fallen into a cycle of bingeing followed by starvation, often admit that they barely taste the food. They eat, instead, to blot out negative emotions, even to punish themselves for being, as they see it, 'fail-ures'. The root of such problems is not in their inability to follow a diet sheet, but in feelings of low self-worth, per-petuated by a complicated relationship with food.

Other factors which can jeopardise the attainment of a healthy weight include thyroid irregularity, which can cause weight fluctuations, injuries and illness, which can make exercise impossible, and heredity, as research shows that a predisposition towards being overweight can run in families.

So what can yoga do in the face of such problems? Certainly, in the case of thyroid irregularity, practise of the asanas can assist the internal organs, including the thyroid, to function effectively. In the case of illness and injury, the gentle postures of yoga can limber up the body and make the person feel rejuvenated and inclined towards increasing their exercise habits once they are well. Yoga also tones up the physique and boosts self-esteem, which, though it will not entirely solve the problems associated with eating disorders, can make a big difference to how the person feels about their body. If you do suffer from an eating disorder, it is vital that you seek professional help. There are a number of eating disorders associations which can be approached directly, though in cases such as anorexia and bulimia nervosa, where the body is at risk, it is important that you consult a doctor, who can refer you to a specialist.

In the case of heredity, the fact is that all of us has an inbuilt 'set-point', a weight at which our body performs best. For some this may mean that they can never be as thin as they would like to be, because their body is simply not made that way. This may be the case if you find that, having struggled to keep your weight at a 'recommended' target, and feel lethargic and over-stressed as a result, this may not be the ideal weight for you. The inner confidence that yoga brings will help you to accept this, and to free yourself from the need to conform to external measure of perfection. The fact is, when you reach your set-point, you have, in terms of weight, achieved perfection.

As for eating habits, because yoga makes you more aware of your body, how it functions and feels, you will naturally feel more inclined to cherish it, and therefore choose what you eat with care. You will learn to read the signals of hunger and feel less inclined to respond to the signals for comfort through food. In time, you may even find that, by way of treating yourself, you automatically opt for something that is good for your body, such as a massage or a swim, than something that is bad for it. Don't feel disappointed if your eating habits take a long time to change. Rather than berate yourself for eating too much, congratulate yourself when you eat sensibly. The following guidelines will give you some pointers towards healthy eating, but the greatest diet-guide is your own body, so take heed of what it tells you.

Avoid overeating

Yoga advocates moderation in all things, and does not demand that you deny yourself. After all, 'a little of what you fancy does you good'. Don't get worked up about the fact that you ate a slice of chocolate gateau at lunchtime or have a big three-course dinner coming up at the weekend; it won't make any difference to your long term health, or weight. The only really important thing to bear in mind is that you do not practise yoga on a full stomach, nor when you are desperately hungry. If the latter is the case, have a banana, which will give you energy, a half hour before you begin. Another good habit to develop is to learn to stop eating before you are full. Try drinking a glass of water (about half a pint) before a meal, and chew your food carefully and slowly. Avoid eating 'on the hoof' or while you are doing something else, even reading, as this will distract you and make you unaware of how your body is actually feeling. Distracted people tend to overeat. Practise the Zen tactic of concentrating fully on your meal, savouring its taste, its texture, and how your body feels. This will slow you down, and the slower you eat, the sooner you will realize when you have had a sufficiency, as the full-up signal takes a while to reach the brain. This is why, when we bolt our food, we often feel suddenly very, very full indeed. Another tactic is to strictly avoid drinking alcohol before a meal as this stimulates an artificial feeling of hunger and prompts us to eat more than we really need.

The gunas

Yoga divides foodstuffs into three different categories, called the *gunas*. These are *sattvic* foods, which are pure foods such as fruit, vegetables, whole grains and milk, *rajasic* foods, which are stimulating foods such as those that contain caffeine and high amounts of sugar and salt, and *tamasic* foods, which include overripe and fermented foods, including alcohol. Ideally, we should eat more sattvic food than rajasic or tamasic, though don't feel that you should make all these changes at once. Instead, try substituting every second cup of coffee for a glass of pure fruit juice, one lunchtime hamburger with a tuna salad. Let the changes happen gradually and the habits will stick; remember, this is an eating plan for life, not for ten days.

'Sattva' means harmony, and eating sattvic foods will assist your body in achieving equilibrium. Nowadays, pure sattvic foods are harder and harder to come by, especially as we lead such busy lives and have less time for shopping and cooking. Try to cut down on processed and pre-prepared meals, as these are generally packed with additives and have less nutrients and vitamins, and more calories and salt, than fresh foods. Look at the labels and select items that are not loaded with E-numbers. Avoid white bread and other over-refined foods as these have limited nutritional value and give your body more work in digesting them, and can result in our feeling tired and inclined to eat more as a 'pick-me-up'.

Salt

Your salt intake should be carefully monitored. Too much

salt in the diet can lead to high blood pressure and even kidney problems. Watch out for it in pre-packed foods and even in fizzy soft drinks. Try cutting down by not adding extra salt to meals at all. You will find that within a few days you simply don't notice it, and that food has a subtler, more pleasant flavour.

Acid-forming foods

Too much acid-forming food is also to be avoided, as it is important to maintain the acid-alkali balance within the body. If we eat too many acid-forming foods, the results can include cystitis and digestive disorders. Tea, coffee and alcohol are acid-forming, as is meat, eggs, cheese and bread. There is no call to cut these out altogether, rather simply reduce the amount, and counter with alkaline-forming foods such as fruit (even citrus fruits), vegetables and milk, either whole or skimmed.

Sugar

Last on the avoidance list is sugar. Sugar provides us with instant energy, by increasing the blood-sugar level. Unfortunately, this high is almost always followed by a lethargic low, leaving us more worn out than we were in the first place. Also, refined white sugar has no nutritional value whatsoever; it simply provides 'empty calories'. Switch to natural sugars, found in fruit and some vegetables and even in milk.

Fibre

Fibre is an important part of any diet, though, as in all things, too much is not the answer either, as this will make you feel uncomfortably bloated and may encourage the body to excrete waste at such a rate that it gives your body little time to absorb all those important nutrients. A case of throwing out the baby with the bathwater! Sprinkling bran onto everything is therefore not a very sensible, or tasty, idea. Instead, get your fibre intake from wholegrain cereals, pulses, wholemeal bread and fresh fruit and vegetables. The World Health Organisation recommends 5 portions of fruit and vegetables a day. This sounds a great deal, but a single apple provides one portion, and you can include dried fruit and even tinned fruit, in a no added sugar syrup. To get the most of your fruit and vegetables, eat raw or avoid overcooking. If you do not have the luxury of a nearby greengrocers', frozen vegetables are nearly as good as they retain much of their vitamin content.

Your fibre intake can also be increased by switching from regular to wholemeal pasta, white to brown rice, and white to wholemeal, not simply brown (which is often just white bread dyed brown), bread.

Fat

We are told to avoid fat, as too much can lead to a narrowing of the arteries and heart disease, but in fact we need it in some degree for energy and children need it too for healthy growth. Again, the watchword is moderation. Choose lean cuts of meat, semi-skimmed or skimmed milk and vegetable cooking oils. The issue of butter versus margarine is a thorny one. Recent studies have revealed that margarines made out of hydrogenated vegetable fats are difficult for the body to digest, whereas it has no problems with breaking down the molecules in butter. Perhaps the best plan is simply to avoid eating too much of either; try buttering only one side of a sandwich, and cutting out butter altogether in dishes such as baked potatoes. You will be surprised at how little you notice the difference. Like salt, too much butter is usually just a question of habit rather than preference.

Meat

Though yoga diets are associated with vegetarianism, there is no need to cut out meat entirely, and it is a good source of protein, which is important for the repair of damaged tissue and cells. Choose lean cuts, and restrict your intake of red meat. Recently there has been much concern about the effect that the growth hormones fed to livestock may have on the human consumers. It is more fitting in the yoga lifestyle to choose organic foods anyway, so look out for organically produced meat and poultry. The demand for such produce is increasing, so as time passes, it will become more readily available. If there is none available, alert your local butcher or supermarket to the fact that there is a gap in the market they could be exploiting!

If you are a vegetarian, you can find protein in nuts and soya bean products, in pulses, seeds and wholegrains, such as rice.

Carbohydrates

Carbohydrates provide the body with energy and are essential for the proper functioning of the brain. Fresh fruit and vegetables, whole grains and cereals are a good source of carbohydrates.

Water

Two thirds of our body is composed of water, and it is essential for it to be provided with a regular supply. Most of us drink too little, and the results can include kidney and liver problems, bowel problems, lethargy and a poor complexion. The bottom line is, you should never let yourself get to the state where you actively feel thirsty, as this is a sign that your body is very dehydrated.

Aim to drink about two litres a day. This may sound a lot, but actually you lose about that much a day anyway, and more in hot weather or if you are doing a lot of physical exercise. Don't drink during a meal as this slows up the process of digestion, and avoid drinking water as tea or coffee. Pure, uncarbonated water is what your body really needs. This might sound dreadfully dull, and will seem like a chore the first few days, but it will quickly become second nature. A way of quantifying your water intake is to examine your urine. If it is dark, then it is full of toxins and your body needs more water to flush these out. If it is clear and odour free you are drinking a sufficiency.

Vitamins and minerals

Ideally, we should be able to obtain all the vitamins and minerals we need from our food intake. However, this is not always possible, especially if we don't have regular access to fresh foods, in which case it is advisable to take a multivitamin supplement. However, you may find that your interest in food and nutrition grows as your attitude to your body and diet improves. Here is a basic guide as to which vitamins are found in which foodstuffs, and what they are useful for.

Vitamin A

This is the eyes and mucous membranes vitamin, and is also important during pregnancy and breastfeeding. Also known as retinol, it is to be found in cod liver oil and liver. That's the bad news! It can also be found in soft fruits like peaches, cherries and apricots, in broccoli, carrots and spinach. Lack of vitamin A can reduce your ability to see in poor light (night blindness) and is one of the biggest causes of preventable blindness in the Third World.

Vitamin B$_1$

Found in green leafy vegetables, such as cabbage and spinach, sunflower seeds and peanuts, Vitamin B$_1$, also known as thiamine, is excellent for promoting good digestion and keeps the nervous system in good working order.

Vitamin B$_2$

This is usually called riboflavin and is essential for healthy skin, and the release of energy from food. Again, look to green leafy vegetables, as well as cottage cheese and fish. Mouth ulcers and chapped lips can be a signal that this vitamin is in short supply. The body cannot store riboflavin very well, so it is important to keep up a regular supply.

Vitamin B$_6$

Also known as pyridoxine, this vitamin is important for the immune system an the formation of red blood cells. It can be obtained from yoghurt, meat and fish. Anaemia can be a sign of B$_6$ deficiency.

Vitamin B$_{12}$

This vitamin is essential for the growth and division of

cells and for red blood cell formation. Find it in white fish and eggs if you are not a meat eater.

Breakfast cereals, potatoes, eggs and avocados are also rich in B vitamins.

Vitamin C
This vitamin is very important for building up resistance to colds, and for curing hangovers as alcohol severely depletes the body's vitamin C supplies. It is also essential for collagen, the tissue-forming substance that pretty much holds the body together. Fresh fruit and vegetables are the best source of this vitamin. A large orange, or glass of freshly squeezed orange juice, will provide roughly as much as you need per day. Vitamin C is particularly important for vegetarians as it aids the absorption of iron from plant foods.

Vitamin D
Sunlight gives us vitamin D, which just goes to show that your mother was quite right when she told you to go outside and get some colour in your cheeks. It can also be found in fish oils, milk, butter and eggs, and is vital for the health of bones and teeth. Osteoporosis, the bone disease characterised by a 'thinning' of the bones, often runs in families. If it does in yours, you are well advised to keep up a good intake of vitamin D.

Vitamin E
This vitamin helps to reduce tiredness, and is found in, unfortunately, brussels sprouts. It is also found in green leafy vegetables, seeds and vegetable oils.

Vitamin F
This vitamin is essential for healthy skin and shiny hair, and is found in avocados, peanuts and sunflower seeds.

Vitamin K
Found in eggs, cod liver oil and yoghurt, this is the vitamin that helps your blood to clot after injury and surgery. This vitamin is also used by the body to make proteins that keep the bones and tissue healthy.

Vitamin P
This vitamin strengthens the capillaries, the tiny blood vessels found throughout the body. If it is in short supply you may find that you bruise more easily than normal and that your gums bleed. Strawberries, cherries and the pith of oranges and lemons are a good source of vitamin P.

Calcium
Like vitamin D, calcium is essential for healthy bones, as well as muscle function and blood clotting. It is found in dairy products, tinned sardines with bones and sesame seeds.

Chloride

This is vital for the formation of stomach acid, though of course, you don't want to take too much. It is found in table salt and foods containing it, and you will take a sufficiency through a normal daily diet.

Iron

Anaemia and fatigue are the classic symptoms of an iron deficiency and can be rectified by eating offal, egg yolk, and dark green leafy vegetables, such as spinach and kail.

Magnesium

Lack of magnesium can cause muscles cramps and even tremors, known as tetany, because it is essential for muscle contraction. Dried figs and green vegetables are rich in magnesium.

Manganese

Eat nuts, cereals and brown rice to upkeep your levels of manganese, which is important for the production of bone and connective tissue.

Phosphorus

This mineral helps to maintain healthy bones and teeth as well as assisting the body to absorb nutrients. It is found in meat, fish, nuts and seeds.

Potassium

This mineral helps to keep the heartbeat and blood pressure regular, and is to be found in fruit, especially bananas, seeds and nuts. Too much potassium is bad for the heart however, so keep within the recommended daily amount of 3500 mg.

Zinc

This is an important mineral for teenagers as it aids growth and the action of many of the body's enzymes. Smokers should ensure that they have enough zinc in their diets, as smoking depletes the body's supplies. Zinc is found in red meat, peanuts and sunflower seeds.

Chapter Ten

Yoga and Women

Body Image

Over the centuries the ideal of feminine beauty has altered. Even as recently as the 19th century women who were overweight, by 20th century standards that is, were considered attractive; thinness was equated with poverty or illness. However, nowadays the ideals presented by media and fashion are ever-changing and often conflicting. On the one hand, women's magazines run articles explaining that diets do not work, and that women should learn to be happy with what they have, while three pages on is a fashion spread depicting models of prepubescent skinniness, many of them are prepubescent in fact, wearing adult women's clothes! The current obsession with skinniness is particularly bad news for young women, whose bodies are undergoing the usually traumatic transformation from childlike slenderness to womanly curves. The message implicit in the age of 'heroin chic' is that this change is something they can control, and indeed should control, if they plan on being beautiful. The result is a huge increase in teenage dieting, which can spiral into such life-threatening situations as anorexia nervosa and overuse of 'slimming aids' like laxatives. It is even partly to blame for the increase in young women smokers (who are now taking up the weed at a faster rate than young men), as smoking is known to be an appetite suppressant and can therefore assist in losing weight.

Even adult women are vulnerable. The ideal of beauty has become very narrow indeed, focusing on youthful skin and youthful figures, but with the added idea that a large bust is essential for women who seek to look sexy. The only winners in all this are the slimming industry and plastic surgeons. The adverts run by these industries lead women to believe that, with all this 'help' available, a failure to conform to the ideal is their own fault. Expensive skin creams are marketed to women with the promise that they can 'hold back the clock', while diets, some of them extremely unnourishing, promise dramatic weight loss. Plastic surgeons even offer lunchtime appointments so that busy women can pop in for breast implants and still make it back to the office for that important meeting. It could not be easier. They are implicitly saying, so what is stopping you?

While not all women spend their lives pounding away at gyms, eating low-calorie ready-meals and agonizing over pictures of Kate Moss, most find that their self-esteem suffers from the constant bombardment of ideal images and 'easy' ways to achieve it. They feel guilty for succumbing, knowing that a moneymaking industry is behind all this pressure to conform, but the pressure is insidious nonetheless.

Compared to the promises of diet programmes and surgery, which offer dramatic change in a short time, yoga might seem mild and ineffectual by comparison, but it is not so. A session under the knife may give you a 36C bust, a ten-day crash diet may give you a flat stomach, but what neither will do is make you any happier with your body in the long term. Which suits the industry, as it can sell you something else in the future. Yoga can teach you how to love your body, how to be 'happy in your skin'. The only difference is that it takes a little longer.

Regular practise of the asanas will tone muscles and also assist the efficient functioning of internal organs. This will make you feel healthier and more supple, and will, in time, bring a noticeable improvement to the appearance of your body. However, this is possibly the least important effect of yoga for someone who suffers from poor body image. Yoga will help you to look at your body in a different way. It will help you to see it from the outside in, and appreciate it for the miraculous machine that it is, rather than as an object on which you hang clothes and could do with a few repairs. Susie Orbach in her book *Fat is a Feminist Issue* begins an exercise for improving body image by suggesting a consideration of just what your body is capable. 'Concentrate on yourself. What do you see? Look from the outside in and then try to feel your body from the inside out. Think of the functions of your different body parts. Are hands merely for decoration or are they moving, active parts of us? Are legs for adornment or do they serve important functions? Try to see the wealth of activities that your body performs and is capable of; try and appreciate its physicality and deftness.'

With regular yoga practise you will come, naturally, to regard your body in a more appreciative, healthier way. Even if, for the first few months, you are still diet-hopping and anxious, a new way of seeing yourself will begin to emerge.

Menstruation

A number of yogic texts suggest that women should not practise asanas during menstruation at all, but this is not true. Of course, you must pay attention to how your body is feeling, and if practise of asanas at this point in the monthly cycle is unpleasant, in any way, then desist. After all, it is only a few days out of your routine and will not set you back. Take care, however, to avoid the inverted postures, as these reverse the natural downward flow of menstrual blood.

Exercises that tone the abdominal muscles help to ensure that internal organs attain maximum health. Postures such as the cat, the cobra and the fish are very effective in this area, and can help to regulate the menstrual cycle, which can go a long way towards easing off the effects of period cramps and premenstrual syndrome. Some women find that their periods become a little heavier in the first two or three days of their period, but the plus side of this is that the length of the period will generally be shorter. If you are at all concerned, consult a doctor, but so long as you are not pushing yourself too hard, and avoiding the inverted postures at this time, there should be no ill-effects.

Yoga is also very effective at relieving stomach cramps. It can also reduce the effects of premenstrual syndrome, by helping to reduce mood swings and irritability. Regular practice will make you more aware of your body and its natural cycles, and this awareness can significantly alter the way you view menstruation, seeing it less as a painful nuisance and more as a manifestation of the body's workings and fertility. It won't necessarily make you whoop with joy when you are due, but it will make it a little easier to bear.

Yoga and Pregnancy

As doubtless everyone will tell you throughout these nine months, the most important thing is to go gently. Don't take up yoga for the first time when you are already pregnant; ideally you should be a veteran of at least a few months. For those already skilled in yoga, the first two to three months should be fine, so long as there are no complications in the pregnancy, as the foetus is still safely tucked into the pelvis. During this time try to locate a yoga teacher who is trained in prenatal care. A yoga-practising midwife would be ideal! If such a person cannot be found, discuss the asanas with your doctor or regular yoga teacher, and always take careful note of how your body feels. Pay particular attention to any bleeding.

After the first three months, avoid inverted postures, anything that involves lying on your front, such as the cobra asana, and postures that involve stretching backwards as this will put a strain on the front of the body. However, if all this advice makes you feel inclined to shut this book altogether, remember that yoga is excellent for the heart and the blood circulation, so is invaluable for both the coming baby and the mother. Also, many women find that the change in their bodies makes them feel clumsy and imbalanced, and gentle yoga exercises, particularly the ones that develop posture, such as the tree, will help to re-orientate you with your altering bodyshape, and help you to achieve balance, while stretching will help to relieve the aches and pains that come with carrying a new life inside you.

One asana that is particularly helpful for strengthening the pelvic muscles in preparation for childbirth is the butterfly pose. Another is the squatting pose. Begin by stand-

The squatting pose

ing with your toes facing out the way and your feet a couple of feet apart. You may like to bring your hands together at chest height, palms together, in the praying position. Take a deep breath and as you breathe out, bend your knees and lower yourself down into a hunkering position.

Remember to keep your back and head straight, don't tilt your upper body towards the floor, and ensure that your knees and elbows are pointing outwards and not pressing into your abdomen. If this is too much of a strain, place a telephone book or even two, underneath to support your buttocks and shorten the stretch. To stand up, reverse the process and slowly straighten your legs. Take care not to jerk upright. This is not only a very soothing pose, it is giving all those muscles that you will need when push come to shove a good work out.

Crescent moon

As back strain is a common feature of pregnancy, you may find that you miss those wonderfully relieving back stretches that you are now advised against. A modified version to try, in this case, is the crescent moon, which counters the frontal stretch with a supporting leg up front. Being by kneeling with your right knee bent so that your thigh, lower leg and the floor form three sides of a square. Your right foot should be flat on the floor. Face forward, making sure that your hips and shoulders are not twisted to the side, and clasp your right knee with both hands. Stretch your left leg back the way, as if you were doing a lunge. If the stretch on your left thigh is too much with the toes curled under, allow your foot to lie, sole up, on the floor. Now take a deep breath and, as you exhale, stretch your spine backwards, your head up to face the ceiling.

The crescent moon

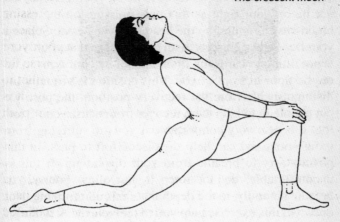

Your back, left leg and head should now form the inside arc of a crescent moon. Hold for a moment and then relax, pulling your left leg back. Now repeat for the other side. As with the cobra, counter this backward stretch with a forward one, but take care not to put pressure on the front body.

The diaphragm breathing exercises are a great way of relieving the stresses of pregnancy and many women have found that they are enormously beneficial when it comes to going through labour. They can also help to rejuvenate even the most exhausted of mothers-to-be. A very pleasant exercise to try is to lie on your left side. Do not lie on your right as this puts pressure on the major blood vessel running to the heart, the vena cava. Support your head and right knee with cushions, so that your body is not tilting towards the floor, and allow your arms to lie on the floor in front of you. This position is virtually indistinguishable from the recovery position, the pose we put people in to help them recover from nausea and fainting. It is also very comfortable if you are suffering from indigestion, and can help the discomfort to pass. In this position, try to breathe from your diaphragm. If this is uncomfortable, do not force it, but allow yourself to breathe naturally, to the depth that feels comfortable. Not only will this exercise help you to feel relaxed, it will also promote better sleep; something you will be in great need of in the very near future.

Many women find that, when they become pregnant, they are treated differently. They may be surrounded by, often extremely well-meaning, people who feel duty-bound to offer advice and instructions on what to do. This can become very stressful for the mother-to-be, and a gentle yoga session, including meditation, can go a long way to alleviating those negative feelings and recharging the reservoirs of patience. Also, particularly during a first pregnancy, many women feel that their identity becomes lost, that they cease to be the person they are. They feel their identity subsumed by that of a 'mother-to-be'. This feeling, combined with the knowledge that the future is going to be very different from the past, that motherhood will change not only their lifestyle but also their priorities, can be inordinately distressing. It is important for you, and your child, to keep in touch with who and what you are, and to feel that the baby is not a threat to you but a positive and wonderful addition to your life. The meditation exercises that bring your mind to focus on your inner essence are excellent in promoting inner confidence and a sense of surety. They can also be used to meditate upon the life growing inside you and to come to terms with the future. Many women have said that such exercises make them feel bonded with their child.

After you have given birth, you may feel tempted to throw yourself into full yoga sessions to tone up your body. You should leave out yoga altogether for the few weeks following delivery, and if there were complications, such as a Caesarean section, hold off for longer. In the latter circumstance you are advised to seek the counsel of a doctor before recommencing.

A note on selfishness

To many of us, the idea of taking up a practise that is solely for our own benefit, and spiritual benefit at that, is almost alien. Especially if it is something that seems so 'woolly' and mystical as yoga. We tend to regard such behaviour as self indulgent and faddish, something we would imagine a Hollywood star taking up, or a New Age traveller. It is important to consider just how such notions come about in order to banish them from our minds.

To start at the very beginning, Eastern and Western cultures developed in very different ways. The West turned its gaze outwards towards tangible signs of human progress such as the sciences and the arts, the building of empires and the accumulation of wealth. It is in the West that many of the great scientific and medical breakthroughs were made, where the great theories of economics and politics were created, and, right up until the 20th century, we fully believed that we were the masters of the civilized world. Even our great religions, Catholicism and Protestantism, had a certain externalised quality to them. We sang loud hymns, recited prayers, and wore our best clothes to parade ourselves on the way to worship.

It was only when Western man began to search in his mind that he discovered the one area in which he was rather lacking; that of spiritual development. Sigmund Freud had discovered that we had another level of consciousness, the subconscious, and though many of his theories are flawed, he was right in the belief that our minds work on levels other than the most accessible, everyday one. After all, here was this previously unimagined storehouse of memories and feelings that had been informing our everyday thoughts and behavioural patterns without us even noticing.

Meanwhile, in the East, the gaze had been turned inwards, looking at the spirit and ways to elevate the consciousness. Little wonder then, that in the 1960s and 70s, when young people were breaking with the traditions of their society, and looking for 'the meaning of life', they looked to the East, where such questions had been actively considered for thousands of years.

Even today, we still tend to rate someone's success in life by their material wealth. We know only too well that money does not equal happiness, but we still persist in the idea that somehow, if we personally had all that wealth, we would be happy with it. It is the conditioning of centuries and therefore very hard to shake off. We still consider it a novelty when someone turns their back on a rich lifestyle to live a simpler existence, and secretly wonder how long they will stick it out before they crave 5 star hotels and a fast car once again.

This externalisation is also apparent in the way that we behave towards others, and in our notions of selfishness and selflessness. We say things like 'Oh go on, be good to yourself' as if we were somehow prompting someone into doing something nice but wicked. This is especially true of women, who often view self-help as an unfeminine and 'grabby' trait. Helping ourselves is not considered a virtue, as we tend to equate it with the idea of doing so to the detriment of others. This need not be so, and the Eastern mystics have known this all along. By helping ourselves, we are better equipped to help others. Think of it this way. If you gave over every ounce of your physical energy to helping other people, leaving none to attend to your basic needs, then how much good would you be able to do when you finally collapsed with exhaustion? In fact, someone would have to come and look after you. Therefore, keeping yourself healthy is a necessary act of self-interest if you are to help others. Similarly so in the case of the spirit. If you are so out of touch with your inner being that you scarcely know yourself as anything other than someone's partner, parent or friend, how can you listen to others, offer good advice, be a good partner, parent or friend? Attending to yourself through yoga is a way of recharging your personal batteries and making you a more capable and useful person.

And here's a thought. Are you not a person too, and therefore equally deserving of a little care?

Chapter Eleven

Yoga for Children and Adolescents

It has been estimated that modern children burn up to 25% fewer calories than children in the 1940s. This is partly due to the advent of TVs and computer games, which absorb a child's interest but require no physical activity whatsoever. After school activities are much more likely to revolve around children's television programmes than a game of football, for instance. Children are also becoming less physically active because of parents' fearing that, left unsupervised, they run the risk of being involved in car accidents or being molested by strangers. Thus, many children are ferried to and from school in cars, rather than being allowed to walk home alone, and spend less time playing out of doors than their parents did as children.

The result is that more and more children are growing up accustomed to a sedentary lifestyle, which means that they will be less likely to pursue physical exercise either now or when they become adults. Lack of exercise can result in weight problems, especially as they are now tempted by a wide and dazzling array of high-calorie snacks, and to depression, a lack of confidence in their bodies and a weaker immune system.

Yoga can reverse this tendency in children by introducing them to a form of physical exercise that is gentle and, above all, fun. This will increase their overall suppleness and make them more inclined towards other forms of physical activity, just as it does for adults. As children are more supple than adults, and have the ability to learn quickly, childhood is the perfect time to introduce a person to yoga. It could become a lifelong habit and will encourage you to keep up it up too.

For children under ten, yoga sessions should be restricted to one or two times a week, in sessions lasting around half an hour. Postures should only be held for about two breaths by very young children. Make sure you leave a few minutes at the end for relaxation. Like drama therapy, the expressive nature of the yoga asanas can be very valuable for shy or disabled children, enabling them to develop a sense of who they are and their own physicality. It will instill confidence to find that they can achieve the postures, and make them feel that they are capable of taking on other challenges in life.

Try to make the yoga sessions fun and encourage children to visualise the animals that they are being. A pent-

up child will especially enjoy being a fierce lion, while
the concentration required for the eagle will help to promote calmness as well as improve posture. The salute to
the sun is particularly enjoyable, especially if it is performed like an elaborate dance, and promotes feelings of
happiness and celebration. Encourage smiling, which automatically produces a sense of wellbeing, and to visualize what they are being. This latter will not only make the
exercise 'come alive' for them, it will pay off when they
are at school, as they will be more attentive and able to
concentrate.

Routine is important to establish the habit, so set aside a
specific 'yoga time'. It is also important to stop when you
feel that the child is bored or losing interest. Long, tedi-
ous yoga sessions could put them off for life.

Teenagers will also benefit from yoga. Many adoles-
cents feel that they hate their bodies as they advance
through puberty, and consequently become moody and
withdrawn. The inner confidence that regular yoga practise brings will help them to adjust to, and understand better, the changes going on in their bodies. Yoga also brings
the added bonus of clearer skin and shinier hair.

Adolescence is also a time when a person is struggling
with their sense of identity. They are no longer children,
yet neither are they adults. As a result they often feel as if
they don't know who they are, which makes them particularly vulnerable to peer-pressure as they fear being

seen as 'abnormal'. Yoga assists them in feeling more strongly about who they are, and what sort of person they would like to become, and this helps them to make decisions for themselves. Also, yoga fosters a desire to be healthy, so will make a teenager less likely to take up smoking or drinking.

An ideal time for practising yoga is in the morning, before school. This is because yoga helps you to feel more alert and better able to concentrate. It is especially beneficial during the trying time of exams, when many teenagers undergo enormous stress. Yoga is good for learning and memory, while visualization exercises improve concentration skills. Furthermore, a short yoga breathing session is excellent for reducing stress during a long night of swotting.

Lastly, yoga requires a certain degree of self-discipline, which is an important skill for the soon-to-be adult, and self-reliance, which brings with it a sense of inner confidence.

Chapter Twelve

A Beginner's Regime

Do not feel that a proper yoga session must include all the asanas mentioned in the previous chapter. You will find some of them more difficult than others, and might want to leave them until you are more supple. Also, you may only have a short time slot for your regular sessions, in which case you should select a few and create a basic programme for yourself. This programme can be altered and added to at any time. There will also, inevitably, be periods when you do not feel inclined towards yoga practise at all. If this is so, then leave it. There is no point in forcing yourself, as yoga must be pleasurable to be effective. Some people leave their yoga for months at a time and then pick it up from where they left off. You might do the same, and it is important to remember that you can go back to it, and that you have not failed by letting it lapse.

The following are a series of suggested programmes to help you get started, but are not designed to be strictly adhered to. Yoga is a very personal thing, and not open to the dictates of others, including this book or a bossy yoga teacher!

A beginner's regime

Before you begin, make sure that your mind is fully tuned into the idea of doing yoga. If your mind is elsewhere, try sitting down with your eyes closed and concentrating on clearing your mind. Try to hold each posture for a minute, and give yourself a ten second gap between each posture to relax and leave the posture behind. Think of how a gymnast, when performing on the beam, closes her eyes before moving onto the next part of her routine. She does this to clear her mind and focus her energies on the next movement; you should try to do the same.

1 Begin with the warm-up exercise which begins from the tadasana posture. Remember to breathe correctly and to avoid straining as you move into the stretches. Take your time with each of the eight steps and give your arms and legs a gentle shake at the end. You are now back in the tadasana pose, so close your eyes, breathe in deeply and, as you exhale, clear your mind in preparation for the next move.

2 Move now into the tree posture (*vrksasana*), the praying position. Locate a spot on which to fix your gaze and remember to distribute your weight evenly across the sole of your foot. Always begin with your right side, and do so for all exercises. There is no mystic reason for this, but it helps you to know where you are in your routine, and prevents you dithering about which side to begin with, which can be surprisingly stressful. Aim to hold the pose for 20 to 30 seconds each side. If you find that you keep toppling over then use a chair to hold onto lightly. Sometimes even knowing that the chair is there, should you need it, can be all you require to maintain your upright position. Concentrate on the idea of yourself as a tree, with your feet as the roots that lead into the ground, and you will increase your sense of security in this asana. Once both your feet are back on the ground, close your eyes, and get ready for the next move.

221

3 Lie down on your front in preparation for the cobra (*bhuhanjasana*). With your hands under your shoulders, lift yourself back slowly upon the inhale until your arms are straight. Think of your vertebrae as like the bones of a snake, bending backwards in unison. Remember to keep your hips and legs in contact with the floor. Try to hold this posture for a minute, and then slowly lower yourself to the floor. Take a few seconds to relax and then repeat the exercise, this time increasing the stretch a fraction. Do not, however, bend so much that it becomes unpleasant. Again, lower yourself to the floor and take your usual ten second break.

4 To counteract the stretch of the cobra, your next move is the forward bend (*paschimottanasana*), which will allow the muscles of your abdomen and chest to contract. Roll gently round so that your are sitting upright, with your legs stretched out straight in front of you. On the inhale, bend your upper body forward from the hips.

If you cannot reach your toes, then grasp your ankles or even knees. If this bend strains your back then you might want to try using a scarf to help you. Holding each end of the scarf, loop it over your feet so that you can pull yourself into the forward stretch. This will help to increase the flexibility of your back and soon you should be able to dispense with this aid. This posture should induce a calmness. If it doesn't then you are either trying too hard or not concentrating. Aim to hold the pose for a minute, and then relax, giving yourself a moment to come out of it mentally.

5   Now you are ready for the spinal twist, which begins as with the previous exercise, by sitting upright with your legs straight out in front of you. Keep your head and spine erect by imagining a piece of string attached to your crown, pulling your slightly upwards towards the ceiling. Begin by placing the right leg over the left leg so that your right foot rests on the outside of the

left knee. Allow your left hand to support you by placing it behind you at the centre of the spine, but don't lean into it. As you twist your upper body to the left, remember that it is your shoulders leading this movement, not your head. Hold for a minute and then repeat for the other side. This should iron out any twinges in the small of your back.

6   Once you have taken your ten second break, prepare for the shoulder stand (*sarvangasana*). If you are menstruating or have heart problems, leave this asana out and move onto the next stage. Before you begin, ensure that your neck and shoulders are going to be protected from the floor by a folded blanket or mat. Lie back with your arms stretched out by your sides and your palms flat on the floor. Allow your knees to rise up and lift the lower body into the air, and your centre

of gravity to shift to your shoulders. Your weight should not be centred on your neck or the hands now supporting your lower back. Your legs should be straight and in alignment with your upper body. In short, your bottom should not be sticking out! Hold for a minute and then slowly unroll yourself onto the floor.

7   To release any tensions that may have built up in your neck and shoulder during the previous exercise, you are now going to do the fish (*matyasana*). Begin on your back and gently arch your back keeping your buttocks firmly in contact with terra firma. Arch your back till your head can be lowered back to rest on its crown, and redistribute your weight so that your head and buttocks are supporting it equally. It is very important that you do not feel that your head is wedged into position. When you are ready, bring your hands up to chest level so that the palms meet in the praying position. Relax into this posture and hold for a minute before lowering

yourself down using your arms as support. Close your eyes and give your mind a chance to clear.

8 Now stand up and place your feet at least a shoulders' width apart in preparation for the triangle. Begin by raising your right arm so that it brushes against your ear, with your left arm flat against the outside of your left thigh. Take a deep breathe and pull yourself over to the left, allowing your left hand to

slip down the thigh towards the ankle. Keep your hips facing forward. When you are stretched as far as you can, hold the pose before raising yourself gently upright. Repeat for the other side, and then repeat the exercise three times. This may seem a lot, written down on paper, but if you concentrate fully on what you are doing, you will not notice the time passing.

9 Now move into the thunderbolt position, remembering to keep your back and head upright. Place your hands on your knees and take a deep breath, breathing from the diaphragm. Hold this pose for a minute. Keep your eyes closed but visualise yourself sitting here so peacefully and still, like a living statue. Take a moment or two to come out of this pose.

10 An important part of every yoga session should be the work-out of the face, so prepare yourself for the cow-face posture. Link your arms behind your back, take a deep breath and visualize that giant clock face in front of you. Without moving your head or furrowing your brow, look up at twelve o'clock and hold for a few seconds. Move to one o'clock, two o'clock and so on until your come right round to twelve again. Now repeat the process in an anticlock-wise direction, taking care to stop at each hour for a few seconds. It is very easy to rush round the clock, especially going in the anticlockwise direction. A good technique for slowing yourself down is to concentrate on visualising each number in turn, and where exactly it is in relation to the other numbers. When you are finished, rub your palms together and cup them over each eye to soothe them.

11 Slowly stand up till you are in the tadasana once again. Take a deep breath, close your eyes and think of yourself standing on the top of a high mountain. Can you smell the cold clean air? Take a series of deep breaths and enjoy the sensation of being upright, of your body naturally balancing itself. Hold for a minute, before relaxing.

12 The final stage, as with all yoga sessions is the corpse posture. Lie down on your back, and let yourself be heavy into the floor. Close your eyes and be on that beach, with the soft sand underneath you. Begin with your toes, flexing and relaxing each area in turn. For the relaxation benefits of this posture to work, it is important not to mentally 'hurry yourself up' so that you can get on with making the tea or whatever. This is your time, you deserve it, so sink into it as you would a wonderful hot bath at the end of an exhausting day.

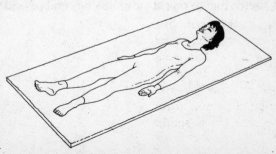

If you are wondering, as you read through this suggested programme, how on earth you are supposed to remember it all, then don't worry, you are not the first person to wonder. Some people like to read out their routine into a cassette and play it back to themselves as they practise. The only drawback with this is that the pace is dictated by the voice, unless you are near enough to the tapedeck to press pause when you feel that your voice is being a little hasty or you wish to hold a pose for a little longer. Alternatively, you can try to memorize the routine and draw yourself a series of twelve diagrams, to be placed somewhere visible, to prompt you as you go along. You will find, however, that you soon know instinctively what comes next, though don't repeat the same routine so often that you become bored with it. Alternate your sessions, adding in new postures or changing the order. Remember, of course, to counter each forward stretch with a backward stretch and to repeat side stretches on both sides.

A Glossary of Terms

Ballet poses are still called by their original French names. The reason for this is that ballet dancers have always felt that the essence of the movements are captured more fully in the original names. This is also true of the Sanskrit words used to describe many of the hatha asanas and the meditative practises. You will notice, if you attend a yoga class, and read other yoga books, that the name for some of the poses will vary. Perhaps this is because the practise of yoga is so much older than the first written collations of it. Whatever, many people find the original names, whether they are strictly correct or not, very soothing and excellent tools for tuning the mind into the activity.

Abhaysa
Sanskrit word for practise.

Ahimsa
The principle of nonviolence. One of the five abstinences outlined in Pantajali's *Yoga Sutras*.

Ajna
The sixth chakra, located between the eyebrows and referred to as the 'third eye'. It is the source of intellectual thought and insight.

Agarigrapha
The principle of non-possessiveness. One of Pantajali's five abstinences.

Asana
A hatha posture.

Asteya
The principle of non-stealing, from Pantajali's five abstinences.

Atman
The individual self.

Bhakti Yoga
One of the six paths of yoga, advocating devotion.

Bhujangasana
The cobra asana.

Brahman
The universal self.

Bramachanya
The observance of continence.

Chakra
A source of energy. There are seven, located along the body's central channel, the spine.

Chakrasana
The wheel asana, also known as the crab.

Dhanurasana
The bow asana.

Dharana
The sixth limb of yoga, requiring the mind's learning to concentrate fully on an object.

Dhyana
The sixth limb of yoga, where the mind learns to contemplate.

Gyana
One of the six paths of yoga, advocating study.

Gomukhasana
The cow-face asana.

Practising Yoga

Gunas
The three different categories of foodstuffs according to yogic diet.

Halasana
The plough asana.

Hatha yoga
The only yoga discipline that involves physical movement.

Ishvara prandihana
Attentiveness to the Divine.

Karma
One of the six paths of yoga, advocating actions.

Kundalini
Literally means 'the coiled serpent'.

Manipura
Chakra located in the solar plexus that is considered to be the source of the 'life force'

Mantra
A sound or chant repeated to aid meditation. Also the name given to one of the six paths of yoga, advocating the use of sound.

Matyasana
The fish asana.

Matsyendrasana
The spinal twist asana.

Mayurasana
The peacock asana.

Muladhara
The chakra located at the base of the spine, and said to be where the kundalini sleeps.

Nadas
Mystic sounds used as an aid to meditation.

Namis
The channels which carry the 'life-force' throughout the body. Chakras are located where the namis intersect.

Niyamanas
The Sanskrit name for the observances outlined by Pantajali.

Padmasana
The lotus position.

Practising Yoga

Prana
The 'life force' or 'breath of life'.

Pranayama
The yogic system of breath control. Means literally 'interruption of breath'.

Paschimotanasana
The forward bend asana.

Prasarita padottanasana
The wide side-stretch asana.

Pratyahara
The fifth of the eight limbs of yoga, involving the mind's withdrawal from domination by the senses.

Rajasic
Food which is spicy and stimulating.

Sahasraha
The chakra situated at the crown of the head and symbolised by the thousand-petalled lotus.

Samadhi
The eighth limb of yoga, when superconsciousness is achieved.

Samprayana
Awareness of all things.

Santosha
The principle of contentment. One of Pantajali's five observances.

Satu Bhandasana
The bridge asana.

Sattva
Harmony

Sattvic
Pure foods.

Sarvangasana
The shoulder stand asana.

Satya
The principle of truthfulness and integrity. One of Pantajali's five abstinences.

Saucha
The observance of purity.

Shavasana
The corpse asana, for relaxation.

Siddhis
The psychic powers that ancient yogis claimed came about through meditative practise.

Simhasana
The lion asana.

Sitali
The cooling breath.

Surya namaskar
The 'salute to the sun'.

Sushumna
The central channel of the body, corresponding with the spine.

Tadasana
The mountain asana.

Tamasic
Foods which are fermented or overripe.

Tapas
The principle of austerity. One of Pantajali's five observances.

Trikonasana
The triangle asana.

Vairagya
Non-attachment.

Vajrasana
The thunderbolt asana.

Vishuddha
The chakra located at the branchial plexus, said to induce fruitful study.

Vrittis
Thought waves.

Vrksasana
The tree asana.

Yoga
The harnessing of mental and physical energy, the mind to the body, to achieve a higher consciousness.

Yogi
An expert in the art of yoga.